Hands-On
Excel 5
Live!

SYBEX Inc.

SYBEX®

San Francisco
Paris
Düsseldorf
Soest

Author: David Krassner
Acquisitions Editor: Joanne Cuthbertson
Developmental Editor: Richard Mills
Editor: Peter Weverka
Project Editor: Valerie Potter
Technical Editor: Ellen Ferlazzo
Book Series Designer and Production Artist: Lisa Jaffe
Screen Graphics Artists: John Corrigan and Aldo Bermudez
Typesetter: Dina F Quan
Production Assistant: Lisa Haden
Indexer: Ted Laux
Cover Designer: Archer Design

Library of Congress Card Number: 94-66290
ISBN: 0-7821-1541-1

Manufactured in the United States of America

10 9 8 7 6 5 4 3 2 1

Table of Contents

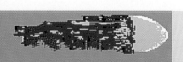

v

Introduction

The *Hands-On Excel Live!* training program offers you the latest in interactive multimedia training to bring you up to speed in Excel 5 for Windows quickly and easily.

Interactive training is the most effective and accessible method of learning. No more stumbling through confusing manuals, no time and money wasted sitting in classrooms. You can study at times that suit you and focus on just the material you want to learn. You can set your own pace, skip ahead, or review material when necessary. You learn by *doing* rather than by watching or listening.

WHOM THIS TRAINING PROGRAM IS FOR

The *Hands-On Excel Live!* interactive multimedia training program is for anyone who wants to learn how to use Excel 5 for Windows, the powerful new spreadsheet application from Microsoft.

For those who are new to Windows, the training program also offers introductory training to the Windows environment— the dialog boxes, screens, and tools common to all Windows programs.

HARDWARE AND SOFTWARE REQUIREMENTS

To install and run *Hands-On Excel Live!*, you need a suitable computer; enough free random access memory (RAM); enough free hard disk space; a suitable monitor; a mouse; and DOS, Windows, or OS/2.

Computer Requirements   To install and run the training program, you need an IBM-compatible computer with a 286, 386, 486, or Pentium processor. The training program will not run on a Macintosh. Your computer needs to have a $3\frac{1}{2}$-inch floppy disk drive that can read high-density (1.44 MB) disks.

Memory Requirements   You need a minimum of 450K of conventional random access memory (RAM) to install and run the training program. To find out how much conventional RAM you have on your computer, type **MEM /C** at the DOS prompt. You'll see a screenful of information, with the third-to-last line looking something like this:

    Largest executable program size: 581,936   (568.3K)

The figure in parentheses tells you how much free RAM you have. If it's over 450K, you'll be able to run the training program.

Free Space on Your Hard Disk   You need 5.1MB (5,600,000 bytes) of free space on your hard disk to install the training program. If you're not sure how much free space you have, type **CHKDSK** at the DOS prompt. You'll see a screenful of information. The relevant line should look like this:

    64,550,912 bytes available on disk

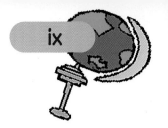

If this figure is below 5,300,000, you'll need to free some space on your hard disk before installing the training program. To get more space on your hard disk, delete some files or transfer them to floppy disks.

Monitor Requirements   You need a VGA or better (XGA, Super-VGA) monitor to view the training program. A color monitor is recommended, as the *Hands-On Excel Live!* screen is very colorful and you will not be able to see the colors with a monochrome monitor.

Mouse Requirements   To run *Hands-On Excel Live!*, you need a mouse or other type of pointing device (for example, a trackball).

Before installing the training program, find the mouse driver on your hard disk, as the Install program will ask you to tell it the name and location of your mouse driver. Your mouse driver will probably be called something like *MOUSE.COM*, and can usually be found in the DOS directory. Just type in its location.

INSTALLING HANDS-ON EXCEL LIVE!

Installing *Hands-On Excel Live!* is fast and simple once you've determined that you have the right computer hardware. You can install the training program from either DOS or Windows. The next two sections of this introduction discuss starting the installation in DOS and Windows; once you've started the installation, the procedure is the same for each (see "Completing the Installation").

Before you install the tutorial, make sure the disk is not write-protected. To do this, look at the top-right corner of the disk. If you cannot see through the little window, you're okay, but if you can see through the window, slide the shutter down so the window is covered.

Starting the Installation from DOS

To start installing the training program from the DOS prompt:

1 Insert the floppy disk in your computer's floppy-disk drive.

2 Type **A:INSTALL** and press ↵ (that is, press the Enter key). If you are installing the training program from another drive, substitute that drive's letter—for example, type **B:INSTALL**.

The Install program will start running.

Starting the Installation from Windows

To start installing the training program from Windows:

1 Type **WIN** at the DOS prompt and hit ↵ to start Windows if it's not already running.

2 Insert the floppy disk in your computer's floppy-disk drive.

3 In the Program Manager, select File ➤ Run. The Run dialog box appears.

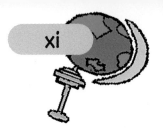

4 Enter **A:INSTALL** in the Command Line text box, as shown in Figure I.1. (If you are not installing the training program on the A drive, substitute the correct drive's letter for the *A* in the Command Line text box.)

5 Click the OK button. The Install program will start running.

Figure I.1

Entering the INSTALL command in the Run dialog box

```
┌──────────────────────────────────────────────────────┐
│ ▬                        Run                            │
├──────────────────────────────────────────────────────┤
│                                          ┌─────────┐   │
│  Command Line:                           │   OK    │   │
│  ┌────────────────────────────────┐      └─────────┘   │
│  │ A:INSTALL                      │      ┌─────────┐   │
│  └────────────────────────────────┘      │ Cancel  │   │
│                                          └─────────┘   │
│  ☐ Run Minimized                         ┌─────────┐   │
│                                          │ Browse..│   │
│                                          └─────────┘   │
│                                          ┌─────────┐   │
│                                          │  Help   │   │
│                                          └─────────┘   │
└──────────────────────────────────────────────────────┘
```

Completing the Installation

Once you've begun the installation from DOS or Windows, a screen appears saying you need 5,600,000 bytes of free space on your hard disk, as shown in Figure I.2. Follow these steps to complete the installation procedure:

1 Press ↵ to go to the next screen. If you don't have enough space, press Esc to quit the installation program, free up some space on your hard disk, and try running the installation again.

Figure I.2

The Install program checks to make sure you have enough disk space for the training program.

INSTALLATION

To run this Tutorial software you will need:

* 5600000 bytes of free Hard Disk space
  for the "Hands-On Excel 5 Live I" tutorial.

Press "Enter" to continue.

Press "Esc" at any time to Quit.

2 Install asks if you want to install a mouse driver for the tutorial. You have two choices:

- ✔ Press **N** if you have installed a mouse driver. Install will ask you where your mouse driver is. The default is C:\MOUSE\MOUSE.COM. If MOUSE.COM is in a different directory on your hard disk (such as C:\DOS), change the directory accordingly. Press ↵ when you are done.
- ✔ If you don't have one installed, press ↵ to install one. Install will ask you which directory you want the mouse driver installed in. The default directory is C:\SYBEX; enter a different directory if necessary. Press ↵ when you are done.

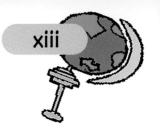

Install asks you to specify where the training program should be installed, as shown in Figure I.3. The default directory is C:\SYBEX\EXCEL5.

3 Either accept the default by pressing ↵ or enter a different directory and press ↵.

The training program will be installed. When the installation is complete, you'll see the screen shown in Figure I.4.

4 Press ↵ to close the Install program and return to the DOS prompt or to the Program Manager (depending on where you started).

Figure I.3

Enter a different directory for the training program, if necessary.

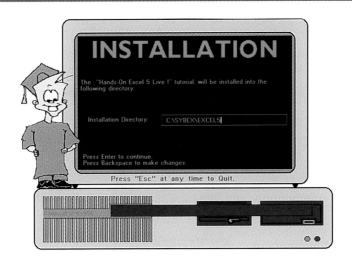

Figure I.4

You'll see this screen when the installation is complete. Press ⏎ to close the Install program.

Creating an Icon for the Training Program

If you intend to run the training program from Windows, create a program icon for it:

1 In the Program Manager, select the group where you want to add the program icon by clicking its title bar. To see more groups, pull down the Window menu and choose the group you want.

2 Choose File ➤ New to open the New Program Object dialog box:

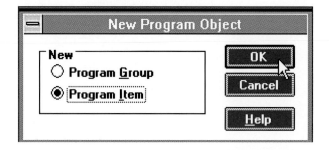

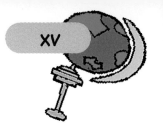

3 Make sure that the Program Item button is selected, and then click the OK button. The Program Item Properties dialog box appears:

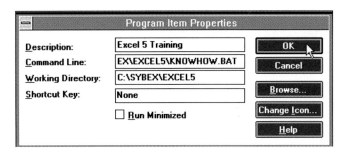

4 Pressing Tab to move from box to box, enter the
appropriate information in the Program Item
Properties dialog box, as shown here:

- ✔ **Description.** A description of the program group.
  For example, you could enter *Excel 5 Training*.
- ✔ **Command Line.** The directory where you installed
  the training program and the executable file that
  starts it. For example, you could enter C:\SYBEX\
  EXCEL5\KNOWHOW.BAT.
- ✔ **Working Directory.** The directory where you in-
  stalled the training program. For example, enter
  C:\SYBEX\EXCEL5.
- ✔ **Shortcut Key.** A shortcut key to the program.
  You can enter either a Ctrl+Alt+*key* shortcut or a
  Ctrl+Shift+*key* shortcut, where *key* is any alpha-
  numeric key on the keyboard.

To find an interesting icon for the program, click the Change Icon button. A dialog box appears telling you that there are no icons available and inviting you to choose an icon from the Program Manager. Click OK, and in the Change Icon dialog box, scroll through the available icons, pick one you like, and click OK.

5 Click OK in the Program Item Properties dialog box.

The icon will now appear as the program icon. You can start the training program either by double-clicking on the icon from the Program Manager or by pressing the shortcut key combination you assigned in step 4 above.

How THIS BOOK IS ORGANIZED

This book is designed to get you up and running with the training program quickly. It is divided into three parts.

Part One, "Getting Started," provides an overview of the training program. It explains the different parts of the program and teaches you how to use them to learn Excel quickly.

Part Two, "Accomplishing Your Goals," suggests approaches to learning Excel 5 for Windows with the training disk. It offers lesson plans for everyone from the Windows novice to veteran bean-counters with plenty of spreadsheet experience.

Part Three, "Excel 5 for Windows Quick Reference," is an alphabetical reference of the most useful features of Excel 5 for Windows. It gives step-by-step instructions for all the procedures covered in the training program and includes a few features not covered in *Hands-On Excel Live!*

CONVENTIONS USED IN THIS BOOK

Some standard conventions are used in this book to make it easier to read and understand.

Keyboard Notations   When you are told to hold down one or two keys and then press another, you'll see the keys linked by a plus sign (+). For instance, "press Ctrl+Alt+A" means to hold down the Ctrl and Alt keys together while pressing A. In this book the symbol ⏎ represents the Enter key.

Hands-On Instructions   Step-by-step exercises take you through the procedures for completing important tasks. By doing the exercises, you'll get the experience you need to gain a solid understanding of how *Hands-On Excel Live!* and the Excel program itself work.

Notes, Tips, Warnings   Where applicable, this book provides special notes, tips, and warnings. Notes, which define technical words, refer you to other parts of the book for further information, or remind you how to complete an action or of where to find things on the screen, have a picture of Luke next to them. Tips, which provide shortcuts or insights for using the programs better, are marked with an arrow and a bull's-eye. Warnings show an exploding firecracker.

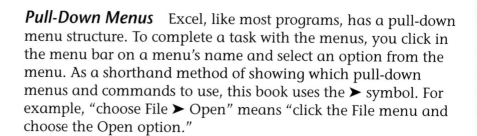

Pull-Down Menus   Excel, like most programs, has a pull-down menu structure. To complete a task with the menus, you click in the menu bar on a menu's name and select an option from the menu. As a shorthand method of showing which pull-down menus and commands to use, this book uses the ➤ symbol. For example, "choose File ➤ Open" means "click the File menu and choose the Open option."

Boldface   When you see **boldface** text in a step-by-step instruction list, it means to enter the text from your keyboard. For example, an instruction that says "type **CHKDSK**" means to do just that.

Part One

Getting Started

This part of the book provides an overview of the *Hands-On Excel Live!* training program. It explains starting the program, the tutorials that are offered, how to find topics you need to know about, navigating the program, and exiting the program.

STARTING THE TRAINING PROGRAM

You can start the training program from either DOS or Windows. If you're using a 286 or a slow 386 computer, you may do better to run the program from DOS than from Windows. On a faster 386, a 486, or a Pentium computer, you should be able to run the training program from Windows without losing a significant amount of speed.

Starting from DOS

To start the training program from DOS:

1 Switch to the directory in which you installed the program. If you installed the program in C:SYBEX\EXCEL5 (the default directory), type **CD \SYBEX\EXCEL5** at the DOS prompt and press ↵.

2 Type **GO**, the name of the file, and press ↵ to start the training program.

3 When the introductory screen appears, click on it to get to the User Entry screen.

 If your mouse is not set up properly, you'll see a message alerting you to the problem. Check that you have a mouse driver on your hard disk, and that you know where it is. Next, either load the mouse driver manually by typing the driver's name at the DOS prompt (for example, type MOUSE or LOADHIGH MOUSE) and pressing ↵, or install the training program again with the correct mouse details.

Starting from Windows

To start the training program from Windows, type **WIN** at the DOS prompt to start Windows if it's not already running, and double-click the icon you created (if you need instructions on how to create a program icon, see the Introduction). When the introductory screen appears, click on it to get to the User Entry screen.

THE USER ENTRY SCREEN

The User Entry screen shown in Figure 1.1 appears whenever you start the training program. The training program keeps track of each user's progress through the tutorials and quizzes. Each time you start the training program and identify yourself, the program invites you to resume training where you left off. Starting where you left off can be very useful if you skip about in the tutorials or if you use the training program at lengthy intervals.

On the User Entry screen:

1 Enter your name (at least four letters) in the top box.

Figure 1.1

The User Entry screen. Enter your name (at least four letters) and your password (four letters exactly).

2 Press Tab to move to the lower box.

3 Enter a four-letter password and press ↵.

The training program offers you a brief introduction to using a mouse:

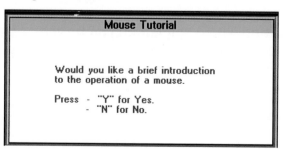

The mouse tutorial gives a short but good lesson in mouse basics.

4 Choose Yes or No. Press **Y** if you're not familiar with using a mouse. The Mouse demonstration screen appears, as in Figure 1.2. This tutorial teaches you how to move objects by dragging them. Press **N** if you already know how a mouse works.

5 At the end of the mouse tutorial, you will be taken to the main *Hands-On Excel Live!* menu screen.

If you chose No in step 4 to bypass the mouse tutorial, you'll see the first Help screen. Click Menu to reach the Main

Figure 1.2

The mouse tutorial teaches you how to move objects around with the mouse.

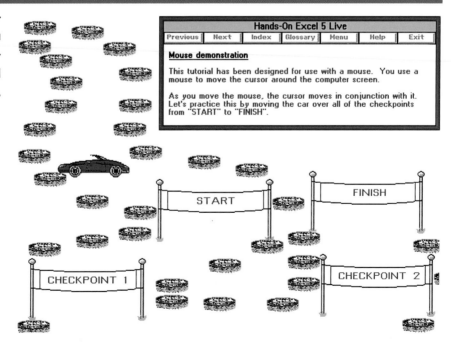

menu screen, or click Next to go through the help screens (discussed in "Getting Help" later in Part One).

CHOOSING A TUTORIAL FROM THE MAIN MENU

The heart of *Hands-On Excel Live!* are the six tutorials—called *chapters*—displayed in the Main menu in Figure 1.3. To run a tutorial, click its title with the mouse. You'll see an Overview screen illustrating the topics covered in the chapter you chose.

Figure 1.3

The Main menu gives you quick access to all the features in the training program.

USING THE OVERVIEW SCREENS

Each chapter in the training program has an Overview screen detailing the topics that it covers. To reach the Overview screen, click a chapter name in the Main menu screen. From the Overview screen, you can either click the Next button to start the chapter at the beginning or click a topic in the list to go directly to that topic.

NAVIGATING THE PROGRAM

Navigating in *Hands-On Excel Live!* is straightforward. All you have to do is use the buttons provided in the Main menu screen, the Index, Glossary, the Help screens, and the text windows. Here's what the buttons do:

Next. Takes you to the next screen in a tutorial or help sequence.

Previous. Returns you to the previous screen in a tutorial or help sequence.

Index. Takes you to the Index screen, where you can look up topics.

Glossary. Takes you to the Glossary screen, where you can see definitions of words.

Menu. Returns you to the Main menu screen, where you can access all the features of the training program.

Help. Takes you to the Help screens, where you can find instructions for running the training program.

Exit. Closes the training program and returns you to DOS or the Program Manager, depending where you started the training program.

THE INDEX FOR LOOKING UP TOPICS

The Index provides direct access to specific topics. It is for users who don't want to go through the tutorials step by step, or who want help fast. To reach the Index, click the Index button in the Main menu or in any of the text windows that has an undimmed Index button. You'll see the Index, as shown in Figure 1.4.

To look up a topic:

1 Click the alphabet button for the first letter of the topic you want to know more about. The alphabet buttons are in the upper-right side of the screen.

Figure 1.4

The Index lets you move quickly to a discussion of any of its topics.

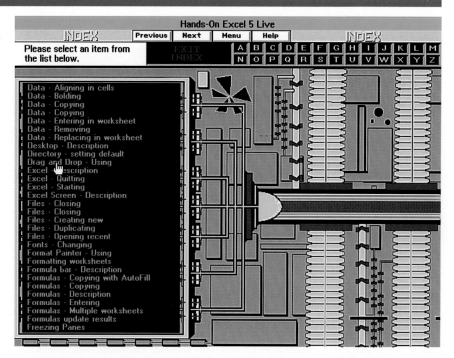

2 Select the topic you want to access. You'll be taken to the screen discussing the topic you chose.

3 When you are done learning about the topic, click the Menu button to return to the Main menu.

To exit the Index without looking up a term, click the Exit Index button. This will return you to wherever you were when you clicked the Index button to get into the Index.

THE GLOSSARY FOR EXCEL DEFINITIONS

The Glossary provides definitions of computing terms. Use it to discover the meaning of terms that you don't know. To reach the Glossary, click the Glossary button in the Main menu or in any of the text windows that has an undimmed Glossary button. You'll see the Glossary, as shown in Figure 1.5.

Using the Glossary is simple. To begin, click the alphabet button for the first letter of the term you want to know more about. The alphabet buttons are in the upper-right side of the screen. Click the term you want to see defined. The definition will appear on the right side of the Glossary screen. Click the Exit Glossary button to exit the Glossary.

From time to time, you'll see *Hot Words* displayed in reverse video—white on a dark background—in the text windows. If you click on a Hot Word, you will see the word's definition, the same one that appears in the Glossary.

Figure 1.5

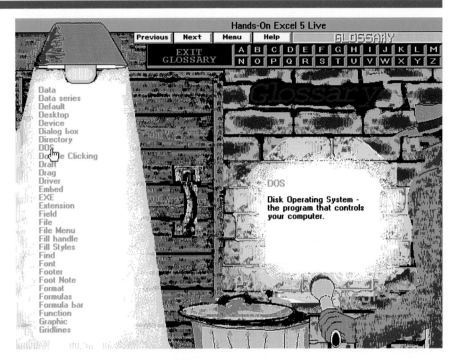

The Glossary offers definitions of computer-related terms.

SUMMARIES AND QUIZZES

At the end of each chapter in the training program is a Summary screen with a synopsis of the information covered in the chapter. Use the summary screens to review the information in the chapter.

You can move directly to the summary for any chapter by clicking the S button to the right of the chapter title in the Main menu screen (see Figure 1.3). Pressing S is a good way to review material quickly or find out which chapters contain information you want to study.

After you've reviewed the summary of a chapter, move on to the quiz to test your knowledge and understanding of the material. You'll see a quiz screen like the one shown in Figure 1.6. To take a quiz:

1 Click on Luke. You'll see the first of four multiple-guess questions.

2 Click the buzzer representing the answer you think is right. The training program will tell you whether your answer was right or wrong.

Figure 1.6

Quizzes help you establish how much of the information in a chapter you've grasped.

3 Click the Next Question box to display the next question. The scoreboard on the right of the screen will keep a running total of your right and wrong answers.

When you've answered all four questions, you'll see a Quiz Summary screen detailing your right and wrong answers.

4 To escape from the Quiz Summary screen, click the Menu button. You will be returned to the Main menu screen.

Click the Review button to the right of a question to go back to the screen discussing the topic it refers to. By reviewing topics this way, you can learn how to use Excel quickly.

GETTING HELP

The training program offers help for navigating its screens and for using the mouse. You'll be offered both kinds of help the first time you start the training program. After that, you can get help at any time by clicking an undimmed Help button in a text window or in the Main menu screen. You'll see the Help screen shown in Figure 1.7.

Move through the Help screens by pressing the Next and Previous buttons, as in the rest of the training program. To exit from the Help screens, click the Return button. You'll be returned to where you were when you clicked the Help button.

Figure 1.7

The Help screen provides you with informa-tion for using the training program.

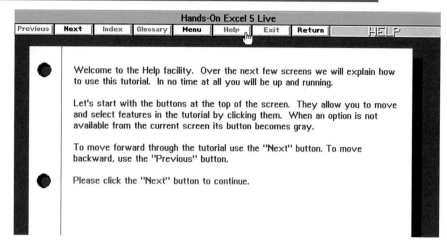

EXITING THE TRAINING PROGRAM

You can exit the training program at any time. To do so:

1 Click an undimmed Exit button in the Main menu screen or in a text window. The training program will ask you to confirm that you wish to exit.

2 Click OK to exit the program, or click Cancel if you clicked the Exit button by mistake.

RESTARTING THE PROGRAM

You restart the training program in exactly the same way as you first started it. The only difference is that when you enter

your name and password, the training program offers to take you back to where you left off:

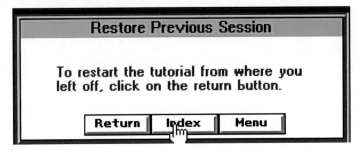

Accomplishing Your Goals

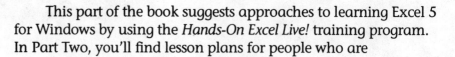

This part of the book suggests approaches to learning Excel 5 for Windows by using the *Hands-On Excel Live!* training program. In Part Two, you'll find lesson plans for people who are

- Using Windows for the first time
- Experienced with Windows, but using a spread-sheet application for the first time
- Experienced with other spreadsheet applications, but using Excel 5 for Windows for the first time
- Upgrading to Excel 5 for Windows from an earlier version of Excel for Windows

Depending on what kind of user you are, turn to the appropriate section of Part Two.

FOR PEOPLE WHO HAVEN'T USED WINDOWS BEFORE

If you're not experienced with Windows, your first priority is to become familiar with the Windows environment, the Windows screens, and the basic operations. Familiarity with Windows will greatly speed your progress with Excel 5.

If you can't remember how to start a lesson or want a refresher on navigating through the tutorial program, refer to Part One.

Start by running the "Windows Introduction" lesson, as shown in Figure 2.1. This lesson will give you a solid foundation for learning the basics of Windows. In this lesson, you will learn how to start Windows, use the Windows desktop to organize your work, manipulate group icons on the desktop to access the applications you need, start applications in Windows, use Windows menus to carry out commands, resize and move windows, use the scroll bars to move about your documents, tell what the different mouse cursor shapes mean, and exit Windows to return to DOS.

Figure 2.1

The Windows Introduction tutorial will quickly bring you up to speed with Windows.

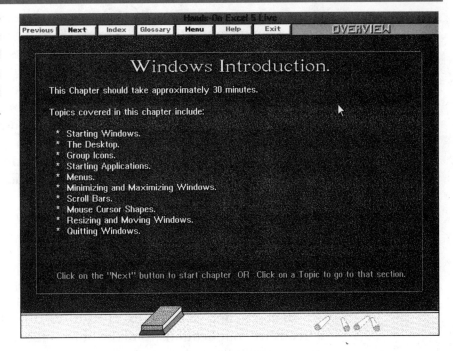

FOR PEOPLE JUST STARTING WITH EXCEL 5

If you're familiar with Windows but are new to spreadsheet applications in general and Excel in particular, start with the second lesson on the *Hands-On Excel Live!* Main menu, "Excel Basics." In this lesson, you'll learn how to start Excel, use the different areas of the Excel screen, select cells in Excel worksheets, close workbook files, create new worksheets, enter data into worksheets, replace data in worksheets, use and copy formulas and functions, use AutoSum to quickly add up columns and rows, save workbook files, and quit Excel.

Once you've covered the Excel basics discussed in the second lesson, go on to the third lesson, "Formatting Worksheets," to familiarize yourself with more Excel features, including opening workbook files, using AutoFill to automatically fill in sequential dates or numbers, setting decimal places for numbers, changing fonts and font sizes to enhance a worksheet's appearance, centering text across columns, aligning data in cells, formatting numbers, using the Format Painter to quickly apply existing formats to other cells, adjusting column widths, adding borders to cells, changing text colors, and using preselected AutoFormat styles.

FOR PEOPLE UPGRADING TO EXCEL 5

If you're upgrading to Excel 5 for Windows from another spreadsheet application, you'll be able to make extremely fast progress with the aid of the training program. Depending on the level of proficiency you attained with the other word-processing

application, you may want to start by looking at the "Excel Basics" and "Formatting Worksheet" lessons to familiarize yourself quickly with how to perform basic operations in Excel. If you're confident about the basics, browse through the later chapters to find the topics you need to study:

LESSON	TITLE
4	More Excel Features
5	Working with Charts
6	Multiple Worksheets and Macros

Use the Overviews and Index as discussed in Part One to go directly to the topics you're interested in. If you can't remember how to start a lesson, or want a refresher on navigating through the tutorial program, also refer to Part One.

FOR PEOPLE UPGRADING FROM AN EARLIER VERSION OF EXCEL

If you're upgrading to Excel 5 for Windows from an earlier version of Excel for Windows (for example, from Excel 4), you'll already be familiar with the basics of Excel and will be ready to move directly to more advanced topics.

Use the Index in the training program and Part Three of this book to discover the features that have been added to Excel 5, then investigate the ones that will be useful to you. Some

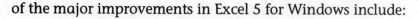

of the major improvements in Excel 5 for Windows include:

- **AutoFilter.** You can now quickly and automatically filter a search to see only the data you are interested in, and then just as quickly go back to a full list.

- **Auditing toolbar.** The Auditing toolbar will help you understand how your cells are connected to each other. The tracing function helps find errors in formulas, such as a circular cross-reference.

- **AutoFormat.** The AutoFormat feature (Format ➤ AutoFormat) automatically applies uniform styles to spreadsheets.

- **Charts.** Microsoft overhauled the charting feature of Excel. The interface has been simplified, you can now use drag and drop, there are now error bars and trendlines, as well as flexible combination charts and curve smoothing. You can also embellish data by pasting in graphics.

- **Database.** Like the charting facility, Excel's database feature has been vastly improved upon. Sorting and filtering are much easier.

- **Dialog boxes.** The tabs in Excel 5's dialog boxes let you select many options inside the same dialog box. You can choose to display the dialog boxes as 3-D objects for an aesthetic effect, or as 2-D objects to save memory.

- **Drawing toolbar.** The new Drawing toolbar lets you draw objects right in your spreadsheet window.

- **Editing.** You can edit directly in a cell. This means you no longer have to work in the formula bar.

- **Format Painter.** The new Format Painter button on the Formatting toolbar lets you format spreadsheets quickly by copying existing formatting to different cells.

- **Formatting.** Longtime Excel users will be pleased to hear that they can now apply formatting to *individual* characters in cells. Previously, you could apply formatting to *entire* cells only. Now different characters in a cell can be formatted differently.

- **Function Wizard.** When you want to set up a function, the Function Wizard steps you through all of the arguments, explaining each one in detail so you understand why you're doing what you're doing.

- **Help.** More extensive Help features include Tool-Tips, identifying labels that appear when you move the mouse pointer over toolbar buttons, and status-bar descriptions of toolbar buttons.

- **Macros.** You can record macros more easily thanks to the improved Visual Basic (macro) toolbar and Stop Recording toolbar.

- **Menus.** Excel now uses submenus, sometimes called *cascading* menus, making it easier to give commands from the menus.

- **Palettes.** Excel now includes a number of *tear-off palettes*. As the name implies, you can "tear"

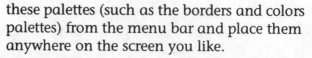

these palettes (such as the borders and colors palettes) from the menu bar and place them anywhere on the screen you like.

🗸 **PivotTable Wizard.** PivotTable Wizard is a boon to anyone who has to do real-world analyses. This function cross-tabulates (pivots) rows, columns, and pages of lists. Pivot tables greatly simplify data analysis by automating the creation of summaries.

🗸 **Shortcut menus.** Pressing the right mouse button now activates shortcut menus of commands relevant to the task you're performing.

🗸 **Sorting.** Excel has gotten smarter in recognizing sort areas, so you don't mistakenly sort column labels and such. In fact, you can now base your sorts on column labels.

🗸 **Status bar.** The status bar displays even more information than it did before, including the function of a toolbar button over which you hold the mouse pointer.

🗸 **Style Gallery.** The Style Gallery lets you copy styles from a template to an existing document.

🗸 **TipWizard.** The TipWizard can suggest shortcuts for specific tasks that you are doing. Best of all, it does this while you are performing the task!

🗸 **Toolbars.** New and improved toolbars speed and simplify your work. You can create (or delete) your own toolbars in seconds, and quickly modify existing toolbars to suit your needs. You can quickly display and hide toolbars as well, or relocate or resize them with a mouse-click.

✔ **Wizards.** Excel's new Wizards show you how to create charts and formulas by using specific templates, automatically setting up the spreadsheets according to the preferences you indicate.

✔ **Workbooks.** Now all Excel worksheets reside in workbooks. You use worksheet tabs to navigate the sheets.

See Part Three for detailed descriptions of using these new features.

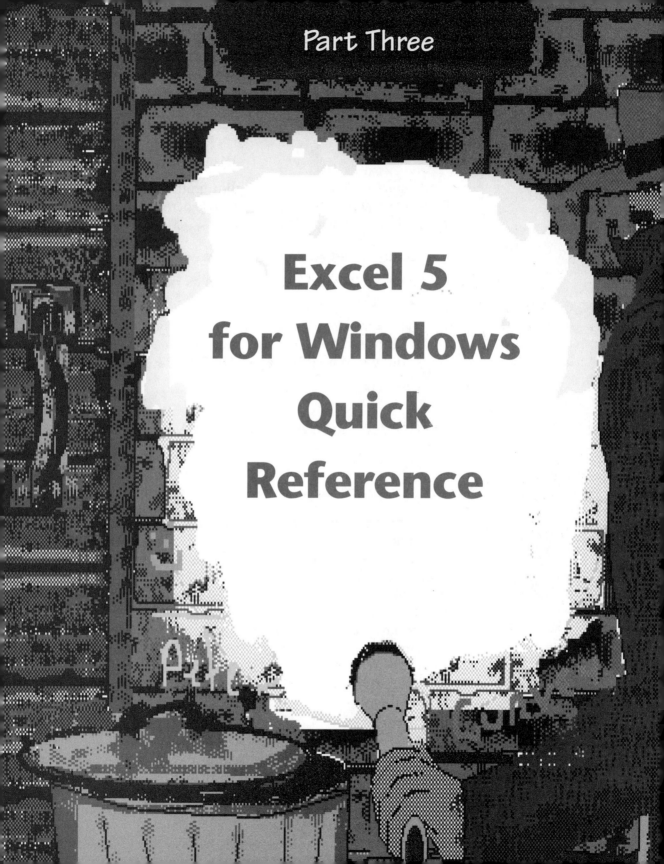

Part Three

Excel 5 for Windows Quick Reference

3D RANGES

A *range* is a block or rectangular group of adjacent cells. A *3D range* is a collection of adjacent cells across several sheets in a workbook. To define a 3D range:

1 Choose Insert ➤ Name ➤ Define.

2 Type a name for the range, such as **JulySales-ByRegion**.

3 Type = in the Refers To box, and then type the reference of the 3D range. For example, you could type **Sheet1:Sheet4!$B$3:$G$8**.

4 Click OK.

See Also   Moving between Worksheets, Names, Ranges

ALIGNMENT

Alignment refers to the position of data in a cell. Right-aligned data hugs the right edge of the box, left-aligned data hugs the left edge, and center-aligned data is centered in the middle. You can align data both horizontally and vertically, as well as change the orientation of text. Altogether, there are seven horizontal and four vertical alignment options.

Excel aligns data automatically, according to these rules: Numbers are right-aligned, characters are left-aligned. You can change the default alignment by clicking one of the alignment buttons on the Formatting toolbar:

To change the alignment of a cell's contents:

1 Click in the cell or select the range you want to change.

If you want to change the alignment for *all* cells in a column or row, select the entire column (click its letter heading or press Ctrl+spacebar) or row (click its number heading) first.

2 Use one of these methods to change the alignment:

- ✔ Click one of the alignment buttons on the Formatting toolbar.
- ✔ Choose Format ➤ Cells (Ctrl+1) and click on the Alignment tab. The Alignment tab offers more choices than the toolbar buttons. Here you can set both horizontal and vertical alignment, as well as change the orientation of text.

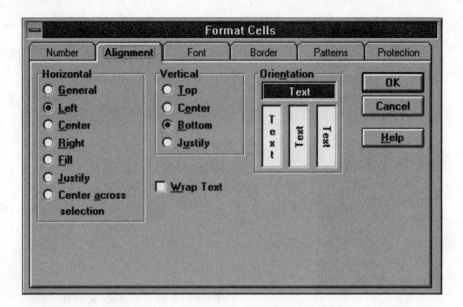

See Also Center across Columns, Ranges, Selecting

ARROWS

A very effective way of graphically showing that two numbers or ranges are related is to use *arrows*. In this context, arrows are simply lines with arrowheads on the end that point from one item to another.

To place an arrow in your spreadsheet:

1 Click the Drawing button in the Standard toolbar. The Drawing toolbar will appear if it wasn't showing already.

2 Click the Arrow button on the Drawing toolbar.

3 Place the mouse cursor where you want the arrow to begin and hold down the mouse button.

4 Move the mouse to where you want the arrow to end (where the arrowhead will be) and click again.

See Also   Drawing

AUTOFILL

AutoFill is a quick and easy way to fill a range of cells with incrementing data. You would use AutoFill, for example, to enter the names of the months across several columns without having to type them in. Or, you might want to have an incrementing list of sales regions (e.g., *Region 1, Region 2*, etc.); again, AutoFill can save you from having to type them in.

To use AutoFill to fill in dates:

1 Type **January** in the cell where you want to start incrementing.

2 Place the mouse over the fill handle (the black box in the lower-right corner of the cell). When the mouse pointer turns into a solid black "plus" sign, click the mouse:

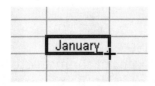

3 Drag the mouse to the right to highlight the cells you want filled. Obviously, dragging over

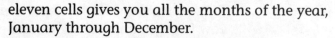

eleven cells gives you all the months of the year, January through December.

4 Release the mouse button and the cells will be filled in.

To use AutoFill to increment numbers:

1 Type **Region 1** (or some such) in the cell where you want to start incrementing.

2 Click and hold the fill handle (the black box in the lower-right corner of the cell).

3 Drag the mouse down to highlight the cells you want filled. Dragging over nine cells will give you cells labeled *Region 1* through *Region 10*.

4 Release the mouse button and the cells will be filled in.

If you go too far when highlighting the cells to be filled in, simply highlight the range of cells, click the fill handle of the last increment and move the mouse to the *left* (or *up*, if you filled vertically). When you reach the cell where you want the incrementing to cease, release the mouse button, and the other cells will be cleared.

AUTOFORMAT

Excel offers dozens of sophisticated formatting options, but sometimes it's easier to let the program do the work! You can have Excel automatically apply one of 17 preset formatting schemes with the *AutoFormat* function.

To automatically format a range of cells:

1 Enter the data that you wish to format. You might have something like this:

	A	B	C	D	E	F
		January	February	March	April	Total
1						
2	Region 1	45000	54900	53444	2626	155970
3	Region 2	26383	62638	26275	37354	152650
4	Region 3	2627	626	6262	7673	17188
5	Region 4	5262	262	3636	8934	18094
6	Region 5	636	363	63636	736	65371
7		79908	118789	153253	57323	
8						

BOOK1.XLS

2 Highlight the cells you wish to format.

3 Choose Format ➤ AutoFormat. The AutoFormat dialog box appears.

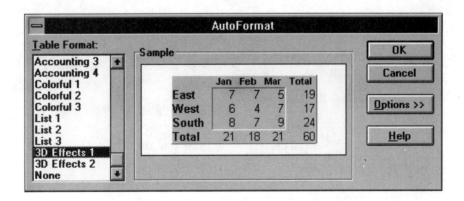

4 Scroll down the Table Format list to find a preset format that you like. You can click on a format

and see a preview of what it will look like in the sample box.

If you apply formatting and then decide you don't like it, you can choose the None option in the Table Format list and click OK to get rid of autoformatting.

5 Choose a format and click OK. The preset formatting will be applied to the range of cells. You may have to click somewhere outside the range to see the full effect. Here I chose 3D Effects 1:

	A	B	C	D	E	F	
						BOOK1.XLS	
1		January	February	March	April	Total	
2	Region 1	45000	54900	53444	2626	155970	
3	Region 2	26383	62638	26275	37354	152650	
4	Region 3	2627	626	6262	7673	17188	
5	Region 4	5262	262	3636	8934	18094	
6	Region 5	636	363	63636	736	65371	
7		79908	118789	153253	57323		
8							

See Also Fonts, Format Painter, Formatting

AUTOMATIC ROW HEIGHT

Sometimes when you change the size of text or numbers in a cell you discover that the cell wasn't tall enough. Fixing this is

quite easy though, thanks to the *automatic row height* feature. To automatically change a row to accommodate its tallest cell:

1 In the row you want to change, move the mouse cursor over the *bottom* border of the row's number heading. It will turn into a "plus" sign with arrows at the top and bottom.

2 Double-click. Excel will automatically adjust the row's height.

See Also   Rows

AUTOMATIC UPDATE

You should give some thought to whether you want the *links* (the connections) between worksheets to be updated automatically or manually:

🖒 Automatic links are updated whenever you open dependent spreadsheets.

🖒 Manual links are updated only when you explicitly instruct Excel to update them.

See Also   Links

AUTOSUM

If you hate having to remember exactly what the command is for summing cells, or if you don't like having to remember which rows you want summed, then you'll love *AutoSum*. With this feature, you can preselect the cells you want summed and

perform the calculation with a single mouse-click! To automatically sum a range of cells:

1 Select the range of cells you want to sum. Be sure to include an *extra* cell at the bottom (or left, if you are summing a row) of the range for the total.

2 Click the AutoSum button on the Standard toolbar. The total will appear in the blank cell you left at the bottom (or left) of the range. If you click in it, you will see something like *=SUM(B2:B6)* in the formula bar.

See Also   Ranges, Selecting

Axis labels

In most charts, *labels* on the axes are a valuable source of information, as they clarify what the chart is demonstrating. The axes are the vertical and horizontal lines indicating amounts on charts.

To add axis labels:

1 Double-click to select the chart you wish to enhance.

 If you do not double-click to select the chart, you will not see the commands you want to use on the Insert menu!

2 Choose Insert ➤ Titles (or right-click in the high-lighted range and choose Insert Titles from the shortcut menu). The Titles dialog box appears:

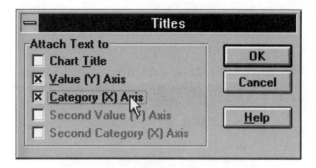

3 Click to select the axes you wish to label. (You can even give the chart a title if you wish.) Then click OK.

4 Excel puts placeholders labeled *X* and *Y* for you. The *X* placeholder label should be highlighted, so you can just type the label and press ↵.

5 Click on the *Y* label, type its name, and press ↵.

See Also   Chart Toolbar, Charts, ChartWizard, Legend, Selecting

BACKUP

To make doubly sure you do not lose data, you can have Excel make *backup* copies of all your files. A backup file is the last-saved version of a worksheet. If your computer freezes or the power goes out, you can always resort to the backup copy of a file. Backup files have the .BAK extension.

To tell Excel to make automatic backups of your files:

1 When you want to save the current worksheet, choose File ➤ Save As. The Save As dialog box appears.

2 Click the Options button. The Save Options dialog box appears.

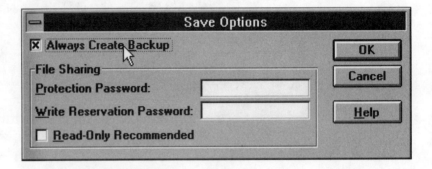

3 Click the Always Create Backup check box. Then click OK to close the Save Options dialog box.

4 Click OK again to save the file. From this point on, whenever you save the file, a backup of your most recent version will be made. It will have the .BAK extension.

See Also Save, Save As

BORDERS AND SHADING

One way to enhance or highlight cells and ranges is to use *borders* and *shading*. Borders are lines around the edges of cells

(you can specify thickness and several other attributes). Shading refers to colors or patterns in the cell itself.

To place borders around a range of cells:

1 Select the cell or range.

2 Click *and hold* the Borders button on the Formatting toolbar to show the Borders palette. If you like, you can "tear" this palette from the toolbar and place it anywhere you like:

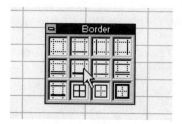

If you simply click on the Borders button, Excel will place a simple border around the selected cells. You won't be able to control what the border looks like with this method, but it is a good shortcut for placing a border around cells.

3 Click on the type of border you want. Excel will apply it to the selected range.

4 Click Close to get rid of the palette when you're done.

To add both borders *and* shading in one step, choose Format ➤ Cells (or press Ctrl+1) to reach the Format Cells dialog box. In this box, you can click on the Borders tab, make your choices there, and then click on the Patterns tab, and make your choices for shading. When you are finished, click OK.

To add shading to a range of cells:

1 Select the cell or range you wish to enhance.

2 Click *and hold* the Color button on the Formatting toolbar to show the Colors palette. As with the Borders palette, you can "tear" this palette from the toolbar and place it anywhere. If you simply click on the Color button, Excel applies the default color to the selected cells.

3 Click on the color or pattern you wish to use. Excel will apply the color or pattern to the range you selected.

4 Click Close to get rid of the palette when you're done.

See Also   AutoFormat, Colors, Format Painter, Formatting

CENTER ACROSS COLUMNS

Often you will want worksheet titles and other information to stretch across several columns. While this is easy enough to do (you just type the title into one cell), it's not easy to *center* this

information across several cells. The *Center across Columns* command does just this.

To center text across several columns:

1 Type the text into a cell in the first column of the range where you want to center it.

2 Select all of the columns you want the text to be centered across.

3 Use one of these methods to center the text across the columns:

   ✔ Click the Center across Columns button on the Formatting toolbar.

   ✔ Choose Format ➤ Cells (press Ctrl+1), visit the Alignment tab, click the Center across Selection button under Horizontal, and click OK.

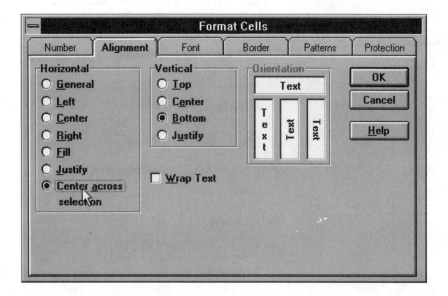

See Also Alignment, Columns, Ranges, Selecting

CHART TOOLBAR

One of the ways Excel makes charting easier is with the *Chart toolbar*. When you create a chart (see the "Charts" entry), the Chart toolbar comes up automatically:

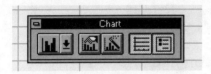

Its features are as follows:

✔ **Chart Type button** When you click this button, the last chart type you used is applied. If you click and hold, the Charts palette appears. You can "tear" this from the toolbar and place it anywhere you like.

✔ **Default Chart button** Click on this to make the chart revert to the default chart type (Column chart).

✔ **ChartWizard button** Clicking this brings up ChartWizard.

✔ **Horizontal Gridlines button** Click this button to toggle gridlines on and off.

✔ **Legend button** This button is a toggle: click once to show the chart's legend, and click again to hide it.

See Also   Charts, ChartWizard, Legend, Toolbars

CHARTS

Sometimes raw numbers in rows and columns don't make a point as strongly as a graphic illustration. For this reason, you can display data in *charts* in Excel. You create charts in Excel using the ChartWizard feature, discussed in detail below. You'll want to use different chart types (which you can specify either with ChartWizard or the Chart toolbar), depending on the data you're presenting. Some chart types are particularly good at representing certain types of data. For instance:

Line charts are good for trend analysis.

Bar charts are useful if you want to compare amounts.

Pie charts are good for comparing percentages.

Click once on a chart to select it. Once a chart is selected, you can delete it or move it around. Double-click on a chart to *activate* it. Once a chart is activated, you can add titles, change axis labels, choose different chart types, and apply other formatting. Here is a 3-D Pie chart:

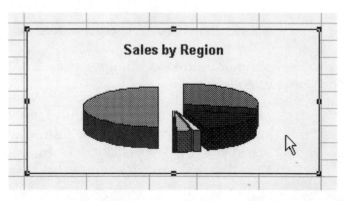

See Also   Axis Labels, Chart Toolbar, ChartWizard, Legend

CHARTWIZARD

An easy way to create charts is with *ChartWizard*:

1 Select the range of data you wish to chart.

2 Click the ChartWizard button on the Standard toolbar. The pointer will turn into a "plus" sign with a little column chart.

3 Click on the selected range of data.

4 A box called "ChartWizard - Step 1 of 5" appears. Change the range if necessary, and click the Next button.

Four more windows will appear, each with different options for your chart.

5 Make your selections as prompted, clicking Next each time until you reach the fifth window. When you are done, click the Finish button. Note that you can click this button at any time.

Excel will create a chart of the selected range with the options you have specified. Click and drag to resize the chart.

See Also   Axis Labels, Charts, Chart Toolbar, Legend

CLEARING

To *clear* a cell or range simply means to get rid of the data or formulas they contain. You can choose whether to clear just the contents, just formatting, notes, or all three.

To clear cells:

1 Select the cell or range you wish to clear.

2 Use one of these methods to clear the cell or range:

> ✔ Press the Del key. This removes everything.
>
> ✔ Choose Edit ➤ Clear and then decide what you want to clear from the cells. Edit ➤ Clear ➤ All clears data and formulas, formatting, and notes; the other commands work as their names suggest.
>
> ✔ Clear with the Fill Handle (see the "AutoFill" entry).

You can also clear cells with the shortcut menu. Right-click on the highlighted range or cell you want to clear, and choose an option from the shortcut menu.

Do not confuse clearing cells of information with *cutting* information from cells—there is a big difference! When you cut information from cells, it is stored in the Clipboard, and you can paste it to other locations. When you clear cells, the info is gone. I mean, gonzo.

See Also Clipboard; Cut, Copy, and Paste; Delete, Selecting

CLIPBOARD

The *Clipboard* is a place in Windows where you can store small amounts of information. You can actually store large amounts of information in the Clipboard, but doing so is neither practical nor recommended. The two commands that place information in the Clipboard are:

- Edit ➤ Copy, which leaves the original data in the worksheet and places a copy in the Clipboard.
- Edit ➤ Cut, which removes the data from the worksheet and places it in the Clipboard.

The Edit ➤ Paste Command retrieves information from the Clipboard and places it in your worksheet.

The Clipboard is *application-independent.* In other words, you can use it to pass data between different Windows applications. For example, you could cut information from an Excel worksheet and paste it into an Access database. You could also copy information from a Word document and paste it into an Excel worksheet.

See Also   Clear; Cut, Copy, and Paste; Converting Files to and from Excel, Insert

CLOSE

When you are finished working in a worksheet and no longer need to refer to it, it's a good idea to *close* it. When you close a worksheet, you simply remove it from your computer's random access memory (RAM). You are not erasing it. A copy of your worksheet remains on your hard disk.

To close a worksheet:

✔ Choose File ➤ Close.

If you have made any changes since the last time you saved the worksheet, you will be prompted to save the changes you made. Click Yes to save changes, No to lose them, or Cancel (Esc) to return to the worksheet without closing it.

See Also   Exiting Excel, Save, Save As

COLORS

You can enhance both data and cells with *color*. You change the color of cells by using the Color palette. (See the "Borders and Shading" entry to learn about the Color palette.) This entry covers the Font Color command, which you use to change the color of data.

To add color to data:

1   Select the cell or range whose data you wish to enhance.

2 Use one of these techniques to apply color to the cell or range:

✔ Click on the Font Color button on the Formatting toolbar to apply the color you most recently selected to the data.

✔ Click *and hold* the Font Color button to show the Font Color palette. You can "tear" this palette from the toolbar and place it anywhere you want. Click on the color you wish to use.

Excel applies the color to data in the selected range.

3 Click the Close box to get rid of the palette when you're done.

You can apply patterns instead of colors to the data, but it looks peculiar.

To add color and other formatting to data in one step, select the Format ➤ Cells command (or press Ctrl+1) to reach the Format Cells dialog box. In this box, you can click on the Patterns tab, make your choices there, and then click on other tabs to change fonts, alignment, and such. When you are finished, click OK. You can also right-click in the range to bring up a shortcut menu, and then select Format Cells.

See Also AutoFormat, Borders and Shading, Fonts, Format Painter, Formatting

COLUMNS

A *column* is a single vertical array of cells. (If you think about it, your worksheets are really just sets of columns. If you think again, you'll realize your worksheets are also just sets of rows. Which goes to prove, too much thinking is bad for you.)

To apply formatting to a column of data in a worksheet, it is usually a good idea to select the entire column. The advantage is that, if you later add *new* cells to the column, they will take on the formatting characteristics that you have assigned to it. However, remember at the same time that spreadsheets are often larger than a screen. So when you select an entire column, you may be selecting more than you know.

Changing Column Widths

You can change the width of a column either automatically or manually. When you change column widths automatically, the width is adjusted to accommodate the contents of the widest cell.

To change column widths automatically:

1 Select the column or columns whose width you want to change:

   - To change one column, you need only select one of its cells.
   - To change several columns, click and drag the mouse pointer over the columns' letter headings.

2 Position the cursor over the *right* border of the column's letter heading. It will turn into a "plus" sign with arrows on the left and right.

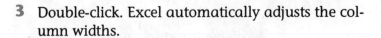

3 Double-click. Excel automatically adjusts the column widths.

To change column widths manually:

1 Select the column or columns (see step 1 above if you need to know how).

2 Position the cursor over the *right* border of the column's letter heading. It will turn into a "plus" sign with arrows on the left and right.

3 Click and hold the mouse button.

4 Move the pointer to the left to make the column narrower or to the right to make it wider. When you release the mouse button, the columns will adjust to their new width.

See Also   Center across Columns, Rows, Selecting

COPY

See Cut, Copy, and Paste.

CONVERTING FILES TO AND FROM EXCEL

At times you need to save a worksheet in a format that can be read by programs other than Excel. There will also be times when you want to read a file in Excel that was created with another program. Excel has provisions to satisfy both needs.

Converting a File to another Format

To *convert* an Excel file to another format:

1 Make sure the worksheet you want to convert is the active one and then choose File ➤ Save As. The Save As dialog box appears.

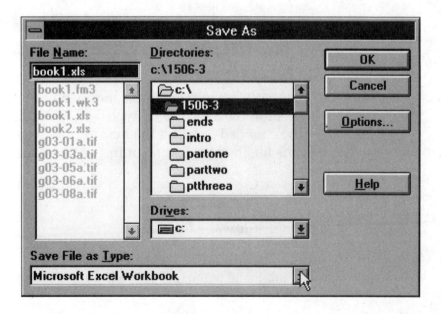

If you want to save the new file in a different directory or to another disk, fiddle with the Directories and Drives lists until you've found the right location. When that's done:

2 Click the down-arrows in the Save File as Type list until you've found the format to which you want to convert the file.

3 Click on the file format you want:

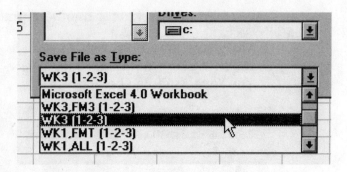

When you release the mouse button, the new format will appear in the Save File as Type box, and your file's extension will be changed to reflect the new format. Notice that Excel still gives the file the same name; it just changes the extension.

4 Click OK to have Excel save the file in the format you have specified.

5 Close the file.

A message appears saying that the file is not in Excel format. Excel will ask if you want to save the file as an Excel file.

6 Just click No.

When you save an Excel file in another format, you are not changing the Excel file into that format; rather, you are creating *another* file (in addition to the Excel file) in the new format. The file you are converting remains on your hard disk in its original, untouched form.

Importing a File from Another Program

Importing a foreign file format into Excel is as easy as falling off a horse.

1 Click the Open button, choose File ➤ Open, or press Ctrl+O. The Open dialog box appears.

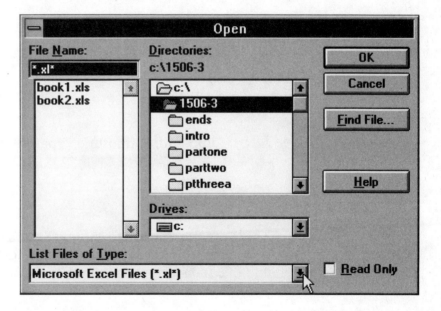

2 Either type ***.*** or type ***.** and the three-letter extension of the file you are looking for, and click OK.

Excel shows you *all* files in the current directory (or all the files with the extension you typed). If you need to, fiddle with the

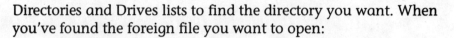

Directories and Drives lists to find the directory you want. When you've found the foreign file you want to open:

3 Double-click on it or click on it and click OK. Excel will open the file (although in some cases you will see some file-conversion dialog boxes).

When Excel saves (or opens) a foreign file, formatting is sometimes lost. Also, if you want to convert the file to Excel format, you must follow the steps outlined above for converting, only this time save the file in Excel format.

See Also   Clipboard, Formatting, Open, Save As

CUSTOMIZING EXCEL

There are many ways to change Excel's default settings to suit your particular needs. These changes fall under the general heading of *customizing* the program and can be divided into two categories:

- Creating toolbars
- Using the Tools ➤ Options dialog box

You can change Excel's toolbars in any way that you please, as well as create your own custom toolbars. The general steps for customizing the toolbars are as follows:

1 Choose View ➤ Toolbars. The Toolbars dialog box appears.

Toolbars

Toolbars:

- ☒ Standard
- ☒ Formatting
- ☐ Query and Pivot
- ☐ Chart
- ☐ Drawing
- ☐ TipWizard
- ☐ Forms
- ☐ Stop Recording
- ☐ Visual Basic

OK

Cancel

New

Reset

Customize...

Help

Toolbar Name:

Standard

☒ Color Toolbars ☐ Large Buttons ☒ Show ToolTips

2 Click on Customize. The Customize dialog box appears.

Customize

Select a category; then click on a button to see its description. Drag the button onto any toolbar.

Close

Help

Categories:

- File
- Edit
- Formula
- Formatting
- Text Formatting
- Drawing
- Macro
- Charting
- Utility
- Data
- TipWizard

Buttons

Description:

3 From here you can change an existing toolbar
or create a custom toolbar:

➤ To change an existing toolbar, click on the different categories to see which buttons have
been assigned to which commands. Click on
a button to see what it has been assigned to
do (its function will appear in the Description
area at the bottom of the box). When you
find a button you'd like to add to a toolbar,
simply drag it to the toolbar. It's that simple!
You can remove buttons from toolbars simply
by dragging them off.

➤ To create a custom toolbar, just drag a button
into an empty area.

To create custom buttons for a toolbar, click the Custom
category in step 3 above. None of the buttons here have
been assigned functions, which means you can have them
do whatever you like. Simply drag a button from the
Customize box onto the spreadsheet. The Assign Macro
dialog box will appear. Follow along as you normally
would with macros. You can delete any custom toolbars in
the Toolbars dialog box.

The Options dialog box is Excel's powerful "control center"
Unfortunately, covering it in detail is beyond the scope of this
book, but you generally use it as follow:

1 Choose Tools ➤ Options. The Options dialog
box will appear.

2 Click on the tab you want to work with.

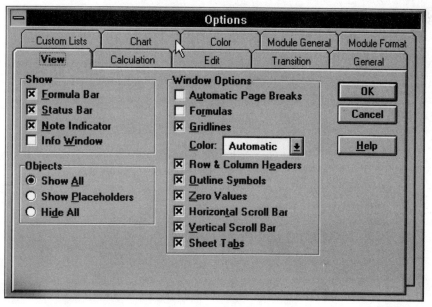

3 Make changes to get the settings just right. Then click another tab and make changes in that category.

4 When you are finished, click OK.

See Also Macros, Toolbars

CUT, COPY, AND PASTE

One very handy feature of computer spreadsheets is the facility to move data from one place to another. Moving data in Excel comes in two flavors: *Copy* and *Cut*. The *Paste* command, the second half of moving, works the same, regardless of

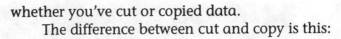

whether you've cut or copied data.

The difference between cut and copy is this:

- The Cut command removes data from its present location and places it on the Clipboard.
- The Copy command keeps the copied data intact and places a copy on the Clipboard.

Do not confuse cutting with clearing or deleting.

> You can also cut and paste with the drag-and-drop method. Highlight the range to be copied, move the cursor to the border (it will turn into an arrow), and drag the highlighted data where you want it to go. To copy and paste, drag and drop and hold down the Ctrl key as you do so.

To cut data:

1 Select the data.

2 Cut the data to the Clipboard with one of these techniques:

- Choose the Cut button on the Standard toolbar
- Select Edit ➤ Cut
- Press Ctrl+X

Even after you've cut information, it is still available to you on the Clipboard (this isn't the case with Clear or Delete). However, the next time you cut or copy data to the Clipboard, the new material will replace what was there before. So be sure to paste what's in the Clipboard before cutting or copying again.

To copy data:

1 Select the data.

2 Use one of these techniques to copy it to the Clipboard:

> ✔ Choose the Copy button on the Standard toolbar
> ✔ Select Edit ➤ Copy
> ✔ Press Ctrl+C

To paste data (retrieving it from the Clipboard):

1 Select the cell or cells to receive the data.

2 Use one of these paste techniques:

> ✔ Choose the Paste button on the Standard toolbar
> ✔ Select Edit ➤ Paste
> ✔ Press Ctrl+V

The cut (or copy) and paste areas must be the same "shape." When pasting, click in the cell that you want to be the upper-left corner of the paste area.

See Also Clearing, Clipboard, Delete, Drag and Drop

DATA

Data is a loose term referring to text, numbers, and formulas in spreadsheets. Often, people will speak of formatting, links, and the other vaporous computer functions as data, as in the following statement: "Hell's bells! The server just crashed like an F-15 with a Sidewinder up the six and I lost all my data!"

Basically, all you do to enter data into a cell is click in the cell and begin typing. If you are trying to create a formula or are using functions, see the "Formulas" and "Functions" entries for tips. When formatting cells, be sure to select them first.

See Also Fonts, Formatting, Formulas, Functions, Values

DATA MARKER

See Marker.

DATA SERIES

See Marker.

DATE AND TIME

You can instruct Excel to automatically place the date or time on a spreadsheet. The nice thing about having Excel put the date in (as opposed to simply typing it yourself) is that the program will *update* the information when you print. Usually the date and time appears in headers and footers.

To place date or time info in a document's header/footer:

1 Choose File ➤ Page Setup.

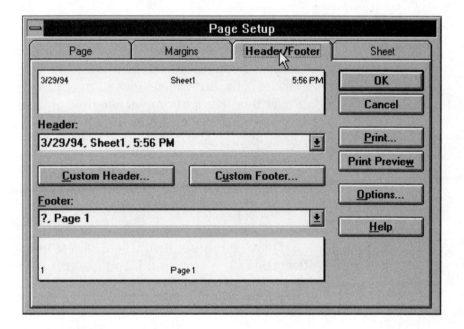

2 Click the Header/Footer tab to bring it to the front and click the Custom Header or Custom/Footer.

3 Move the cursor to the section where you want the info to go and click the Date and Time

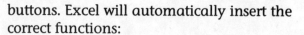

buttons. Excel will automatically insert the correct functions:

&[Date]   &[Time]

4 Click OK twice to close both the custom and Page Setup dialog boxes.

See Also   Headers and Footers

DELETE

The *Delete* key is similar to the Clear command, but broader in scope. If you select cells and press the Delete key, you will clear the cells. But Delete does so much more...

While Clear can only delete the contents of cells, Delete is effective in a variety of situations when you are editing in the formula bar. To delete data in the formula bar:

1 Place the cursor to the left of the character you want to get rid of, or select several characters.

2 Press Delete.

There is another meaning of *delete* in Excel: The Edit menu offers the Delete command. You use this command to get rid of columns or rows, a cell, or a range.

To delete columns or rows:

1 Select the column by its letter heading or the row by its number heading.

2 Choose Edit ➤ Delete. The column or row will disappear for good.

Do not confuse deleting columns and rows with hiding them (discussed in the "Hide" entry). Deleting gets rid of data permanently.

See Also   Clearing; Cut, Copy, and Paste; Hide; Insert

DRAG AND DROP

Excel's *drag and drop* function is simply a shortcut method of moving information. With this method, data is not placed on the Clipboard, and the cut (or copy) is made directly. To use drag and drop:

1 Select the cell or range you wish to move.

2 Move the cursor to somewhere on the *edge* of the range. It will turn into an arrowhead.

⊃n 2	2ხ3ხ3	ხ2ხ3ხ	2ხ.
⊃n 3	2627	62ხ	6։
⊃n 4	5262	262	3ხ
⊃n 5	636	363	63ხ
	7990ឣ	11ឣ789	153

Another technique for moving data is to use the *right* mouse button. When the data reaches its new home, a shortcut menu will appear, allowing you to Move or Copy the range (or take one of several other options).

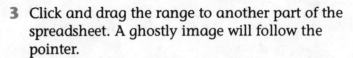

3 Click and drag the range to another part of the spreadsheet. A ghostly image will follow the pointer.

4 When you release the mouse button, the data will move to its new home, just as if you had cut and pasted.

If you want to copy the data as opposed to relocating it, hold down Ctrl while you do the click and drag (a small "plus" sign will appear next to the arrowhead).

To use drag and drop, it must be enabled. To enable drag and drop, choose Tools ➤ Options. In the Options dialog box, click on the Edit tab to bring it to the front. Then click the box next to the Allow Cell Drag and Drop option. Click OK to close the Options dialog box.

See Also Cut, Copy, and Paste

DRAWING

You can enhance your worksheets and satisfy those artistic urges by creating *drawings*. Often, the drawing tools are used for mundane things like arrows, boxes, and the occasional ellipse. But don't let that stop you! Express yourself! Illustrate your worksheets like there's no tomorrow!

To create drawings:

1 Click the Drawing button on the Standard toolbar. The Drawing toolbar appears.

2 Click on one of the tools to select it and start drawing in the worksheet. Click on other tools to use them.

3 To delete or move drawn items, you must first select them.

See Also   Arrows

ERASING

See Clearing, Deleting.

EXITING EXCEL

Exiting Excel is different from just closing a worksheet. When you exit the program, you are taking the entire application out of memory. Often you will close programs to free up random access memory (RAM), which is always at a premium, so that other programs can use it. All worksheets will close along with Excel when you exit it. If you have made changes to worksheets but you haven't saved them, you will be given a chance to save them before exiting.

To exit Excel, use one of these techniques:

✔ Choose File ➤ Exit.

✔ Double-click the Close box in the top-left corner of the application window.

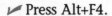

✔ Press Alt+F4.

See Also Close, Save, Save As

FILE CONVERSION

See Converting Files to and from Excel.

FILL HANDLE

The *fill handle* is the little black box in the lower-right corner of selected cells or ranges. Even blank cells have fill handles. You can tell when the cursor is over a fill handle because the mouse pointer turns into a solid black "plus" sign. The fill handle has two functions:

✔ When you drag down or to the right, cells are filled.

✔ When you drag up or to the left, cells are cleared.

See Also AutoFill, Clearing, Data, Formatting

FIND

See Go To, Search.

FONTS

What *fonts* are can be confusing. To a typesetter, a font is a *typeface* in a specific size with specific attributes. For the purposes of computer programs, however, a font is the typeface itself pure and simple, irrespective of size or formatting.

In Excel, the font is the typeface you choose to represent the text and numbers in your worksheets. You can assign the font in a number of different ways. For each method (except Format Painter), you must select data before you can change the font it is displayed in. Following are techniques for changing fonts:

✔ **The Font menu** The easiest way to change a font is with the Font menu on the Formatting toolbar. Click the down-arrow to see a list of fonts and then click on the one you desire:

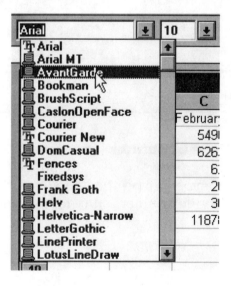

You can change the size this way as well, using the Size menu to the right of the Font menu.

✔ **The Format Cells dialog box** The best way to change a whole bunch of attributes (including font, size, underline, and color) is in the Format Cells dialog box. Choose Format ➤ Cells (or press Ctrl+1) and click the Font tab. Here you can make a variety of changes and preview them as you go.

✔ **AutoFormat** Use AutoFormat (as described in the "AutoFormat" entry) to apply font and other formatting. Choose Format ➤ AutoFormat to use this utility.

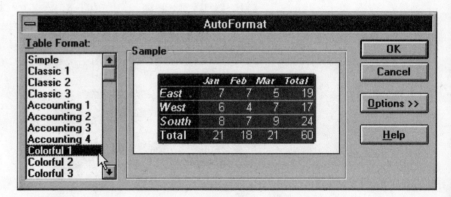

✔ **Format painter** The Format Painter is a handy way to convey formatting information from one range of data to another. See the "Format Painter" entry for information.

See Also AutoFormat, Format Painter, Formatting

FOOTERS

See Headers and Footers.

FORMAT PAINTER

The *Format Painter* does precisely what its name implies: it applies formatting to cells that you "paint" with its cunning little brush. To use Format Painter:

1 Select the cells whose format you wish to copy.

2 Click the Format Painter button on the Standard toolbar. The Pointer will change into a "plus" sign with a paintbrush.

A	B	C	D	E	F
	January	February	March	April	Total
Region 1	45000	54900	53444	2626	155970
Region 2	26393	62638	36375	37354	152650

3 Click and hold down the mouse button and "paint" over any cells you wish to assume the formatting of the cells you selected. When you release the mouse button, the painted cells will take on the formatting of the original ones.

See Also AutoFormat, Fonts, Formatting

FORMATTING

Excel offers dozens of sophisticated *formatting* options so you can make the data in your spreadsheets more presentable or aesthetically pleasing. Excel has five basic format categories:

✔ Number, which controls how numbers appear

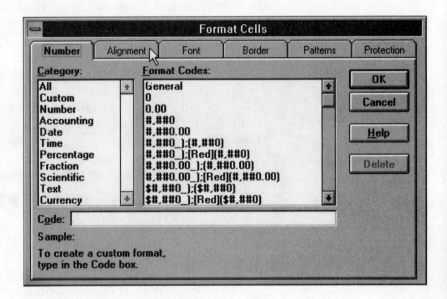

✔ Alignment, which controls where text is in relation to cell borders

Format Cells

| Number | **Alignment** | Font | Border | Patterns | Protection |

Horizontal
- ○ General
- ○ Left
- ○ Center
- ○ Right
- ○ Fill
- ○ Justify
- ○ Center across selection

Vertical
- ○ Top
- ○ Center
- ● Bottom
- ○ Justify

☐ Wrap Text

Orientation

Text

T e x t | Text | Text

OK
Cancel
Help

✔ Font, which controls style, size, underline and color

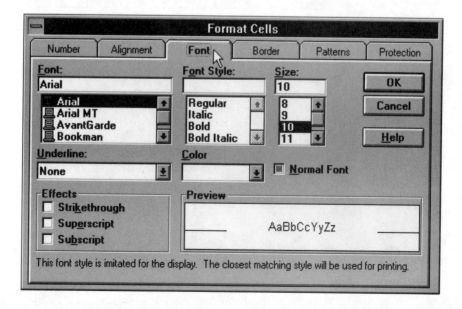

Format Cells

| Number | Alignment | Font | Border | Patterns | Protection |

Font:
Arial

Arial
Arial MT
AvantGarde
Bookman

Font Style:

Regular
Italic
Bold
Bold Italic

Size:
10

8
9
10
11

OK
Cancel
Help

Underline:
None

Color

▨ Normal Font

Effects
- ☐ Strikethrough
- ☐ Superscript
- ☐ Subscript

Preview

AaBbCcYyZz

This font style is imitated for the display. The closest matching style will be used for printing.

✔ Border, which controls the positioning and style of the borders around cells

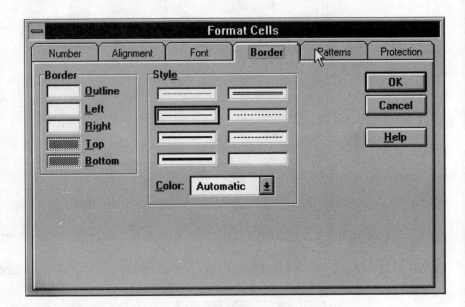

✔ Patterns, which controls cell shading or color

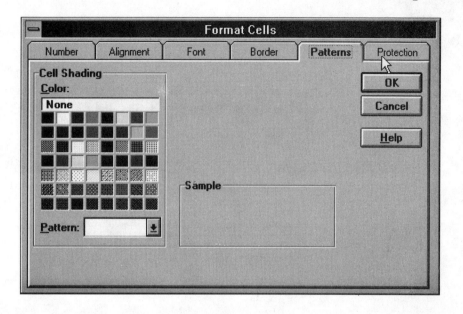

 Sometimes worksheet protection is considered formatting. Worksheet protection is discussed separately in the "Protecting Worksheets" entry. Protection is qualitatively different from other formatting, in that it does not change the appearance of data.

All cell formatting options can be found in the Format Cells dialog box. To apply formatting:

1 Select the cell or range you wish to change.

2 Choose Format ➤ Cells (or press Ctrl+1). The Format Cells dialog box appears:

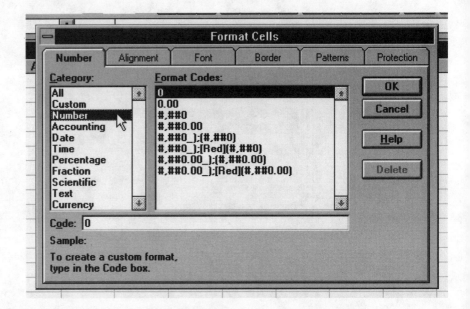

3 Click on the various tabs to bring them to the front, and choose the formatting options you wish to apply.

4 When you are finished, click OK and Excel will apply the formatting to the selected cells.

You can also do a lot of formatting right from the Formatting toolbar. For example, click on the Italic button to apply italics to any selected cells.

In Excel 5, you can now apply formatting to individual elements of a cell, whereas before you had to apply formats to the entire cell. To see how this works:

1 Type the phrase **Sales were up by 25% last month** in a cell.

2 Highlight the figure *25%*.

3 Click on the Bold button. Notice that just the *25%* is boldfaced, while the rest remains in the regular font.

See Also Alignment, AutoFormat, Borders and Shading, Center across Columns, Colors, Fonts, Format Painter, Protecting Worksheets

FORMULA BAR

The *formula bar* is the area near the top of the screen where you enter and edit the contents of cells. You can show or hide the formula bar by choosing View ➤ Formula Bar. A check mark next to its name indicates it's showing.

Running across, left to right, the formula bar's functions are as follows:

Name box You can assign names to cells or ranges in a worksheet and then go to them from here. To do so, select the cell or range, choose Insert ➤ Name ➤ Define, and type in a name.

Then click the arrow in the name box when you want to find the named region:

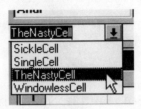

⊠ **Cancel box** You can click this box at any time to cancel your entry. Anything you typed into the entry area will be deleted and you'll return to the worksheet.

☑ **Enter box** Clicking this box is the same as pressing ↵ on the keyboard. By doing so, you're telling Excel that the contents of the entry area are correct (for now) and you want to move on to bigger and better things.

Function Wizard Brings up the Function Wizard, discussed in the "Function Wizard" entry.

Entry area This is where you type what you want to be the contents of a cell. To edit or reformat that data in a cell, select it and edit it in the entry area.

 When you've finished entering data in the entry area, you can place the data in your worksheet by pressing ↓, ↑, ←, or → as well as by pressing ↵. Pressing ↓ also moves down to the next cell, and pressing ↑ moves up one cell. Pressing ← or → move one cell to the left or right. Clicking the Enter box leaves you in the same cell.

See Also Formulas, Function Wizard

FORMULAS

In Excel, *formulas* are mathematical expressions that you can use to analyze data. A formula can be as simple as the summing of two cells or as complex as logarithmic computations performed on many ranges over several worksheets.

To insert a formula:

1 Click the cell where you want the formula to go.

2 Type = (an equals sign).

3 Enter the formula, including any cells to be used in it.

To enter formulas, you can either type the names of cells or click them to have Excel enter the names automatically. If you are unsure of how to enter formulas, click the Function Wizard button, which will guide you through creating a formula.

4 Press Enter or click the Enter box.

The "Functions" entry lists a number of common functions that you can use to build formulas.

In the formula bar, you will always see a formula that is in a cell. But Excel has two ways of displaying the cell itself: it can show either the result of the formula or the formula itself. Generally, you will want to see the result (the default). To see the formula, choose Tools ➤ Options, and in the View tab, click the Formulas option in the Window Options list.

See Also Formula Bar, Function Wizard, Functions

FREEZING PANES

If you aren't familiar with the concept of splitting a worksheet into panes, you may wish to refer to the "Splitting Windows" entry. Once you have split a window, you often need to scroll one pane while keeping the other in the same place. The way to do this is to *freeze* one pane.

To freeze a pane:

➤ Choose Window ➤ Freeze Panes. That's all there is to it!

To unfreeze the panes, choose Window ➤ Unfreeze panes.

See Also Splitting Windows

FUNCTION WIZARD

The painless way to create formulas is to use the Function Wizard. To use the Function Wizard:

1 Click the cell where you want the formula to go.

 2 Click the Function Wizard button in the Standard toolbar. A dialog box appears called "Function Wizard - Step 1 of 2."

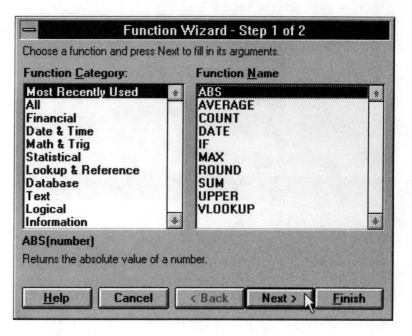

3 Scroll the Function Category to find the kind of function you want; then scroll the Function Name list to find the specific function.

4 When you have found it, click on it and click Next.

The next dialog box appears, asking you to specify the arguments for the function. The *arguments* are just the numbers or the ranges you want the function to operate on.

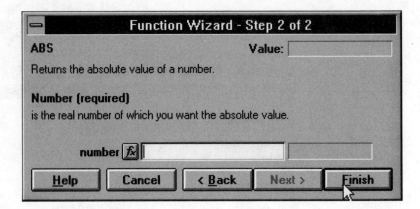

5 Type in the arguments. You can select cells in the worksheet to automatically add ranges.

6 Click the Finish button and your formula will appear in the entry area of the formula bar. The result will show in the selected cell.

See Also   Formula Bar, Formulas, Functions

FUNCTIONS

Do not confuse *functions* with formulas. A formula is a mathematical expression for analyzing data; a function is a single mathematical process used within a formula to make calculations. A formula can contain more than one function.

Common Excel Functions

Following is a list of some of the more common functions in Excel. Note that in most cases, formulas take the form *function*(x), where *x* is a number, or *function(nx:my)*, where *nx:my* represents a range of cells.

FUNCTION	OPERATOR
Addition/Subtraction	SUM, +, *or* –
Multiplication/Division	PRODUCT, *, *or* /
Exponent	POWER *or* ^
Square root	SQRT
Logarithm/natural logarithm	LOG/LN
Find average	AVERAGE
Date/Time	DATE/TIME
Rounding off	ROUND
Future/present value of an investment	FV/PV

See Also   Formula Bar, Formulas, Function Wizard

GO TO

A slick way to move around worksheets is to use the *Go To* command. This command lets you specify the cell, range, or named region of the worksheet where you want to move the highlight.

To use Go To:

1 Choose Edit ➤ Go To (or press F5). The Go To dialog box appears:

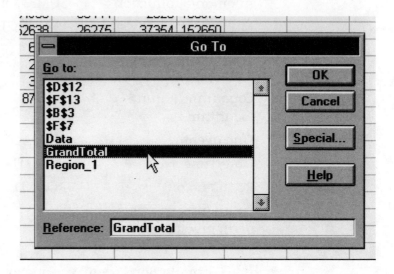

2 Here you have several options. You can type a specific cell, named region, or range in the Reference box, or you can click on one of the items in the Go To list.

3 Once you have made your choice, click OK, and the cell or range you specified will be highlighted.

 A quicker way to move to named regions is to use the Name box in the formula bar. Just click the arrow in the Name box to find the named region. Of course, the region you want to visit must be named, first. To name a range, select it, choose Insert ➤ Name ➤ Define, and type in a name.

See Also   Formula Bar, Names, Search, Selecting

GRAPHICS

See Drawing.

GRIDLINES

Gridlines are the lines on a chart that demarcate the data on either the x or the y axis. The purpose of gridlines is to make it easier for people reading the graph to see what levels the data represent. Gridlines can run either horizontally or vertically.

To manipulate gridlines on a chart:

1 Double-click the chart to select it.

2 Choose Insert ➤ Gridlines. The Gridlines dialog box appears.

3 Make your choices in this dialog box.

 You can have either horizontal (y axis) or vertical (x axis) gridlines. Horizontal gridlines are added by default. You can even have *minor gridlines*, which are additional lines (lighter in shade) to further assist the viewer. These often make a chart look

cluttered, though. Alternatively, you can toggle horizontal grid-lines on and off by clicking the Horizontal Gridlines button on the Chart toolbar.

4 Click OK, and the gridlines you requested will be added to your chart.

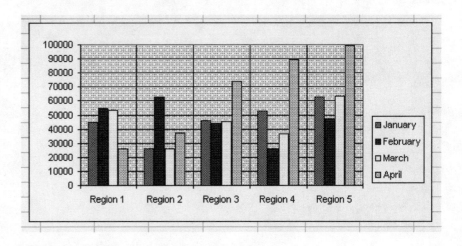

See Also Charts

HEADERS AND FOOTERS

A good way to have information repeat on each printed page of a worksheet is to place it in either *headers* or *footers*. Headers and footers are areas at the top and bottom of work-sheets reserved for things like worksheet titles, the date, page numbers, author names, etc.

To place information in headers or footers:

1 Choose File ➤ Print Preview or click the Print Preview button on the Standard toolbar. The view will change to Print Preview.

2 Click the Setup button at the top of the page to bring up the Page Setup dialog box.

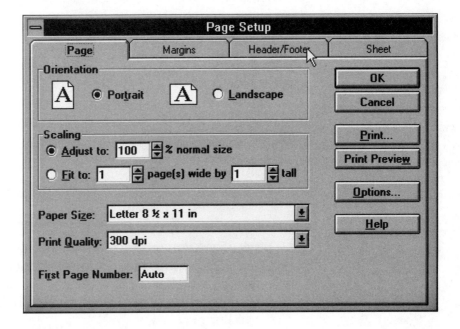

You can reach the Page Setup box directly from a worksheet by choosing File ➤ Page Setup. I recommend going into Print Preview first, though, because you can see what your headers and footers will look like in Print Preview, making it easier to tell how the printed document will actually look.

3 Click the Header/Footer tab to bring it to the front.

4 To create a custom header or footer, click the Custom Header or Custom Footer button. The corresponding dialog box appears.

5 Move into the section where you want information to go. Then either click on icons to place functions or type them in. When you are finished, click OK.

6 Click on the Margins tab to bring it forward. Notice the box called From Edge in the lower-left corner of the tab:

```
From Edge
Header:  0.5
Footer:  0.5
```

This is where you tell Excel where on the page to place the header and footer. Make changes as you see fit; you can see how the document will look in the Preview area. Finally, click OK to return to Print Preview.

7 At this point, you can either return to your worksheet by clicking Close or print the worksheet by clicking Print. Either way, when you eventually print the document, the headers and footers you have specified will appear on the printed sheet.

See Also Date and Time, Page Numbering, Print Preview

HELP

Excel has a massive *help* utility to assist you in navigating the program. There are basically four ways to access Help:

✔ Press F1 to see the Help Contents. From here, you just click on the topics you wish to know more about. Shift+F1 brings up *context-sensitive* help, in which case Excel goes directly to Help files on the task that you are doing.

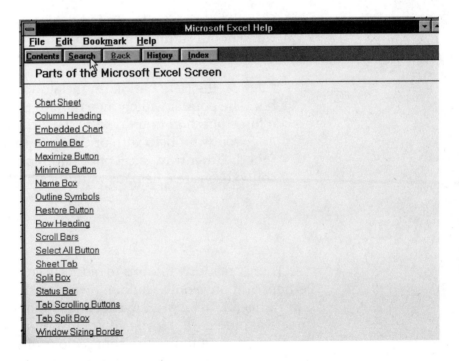

✔ Choose one of the items on the Help menu. Contents brings up the Help Contents, as above; Search for Help on brings up a dialog box where you can type in topics and go to them with a

single mouse-click; Index brings up a full index of all the topics in the Help file—scroll the list and click on topics to view them. The other menu items are self-explanatory.

🖱 Most if not all dialog boxes have a help button:

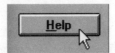

Click it to bring up the Help function. The nice thing about summoning Help in this way is that it is context-sensitive.

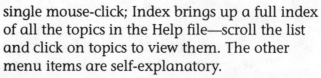

🖱 Click on the Help button on the Standard toolbar. The pointer will change into an arrow with a large question mark next to it. Click on the item you want help with or choose a menu command. Either way, Excel once again brings up context-sensitive help, as explained above.

HIDE

There are many reasons to *hide* cells, rows, and columns. Perhaps you have data you don't want to show when you print a worksheet. Maybe you have formulas that aren't important to understanding data. Maybe you're just plain sneaky. Whatever the case, you can make it so that regions of your worksheets are hidden from view, either on screen, on printouts, or both.

To hide a cell or range:

1 Select the cell or range.

2 Choose Format ➤ Cells (or press Ctrl+1) to bring up the Format Cells dialog box.

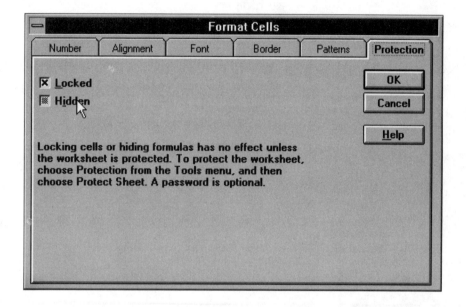

3 Click the Protection tab to bring it to the front.
4 Click the box next to Hidden to hide the cell or range.
5 Click OK.

In order for the cell or range to be hidden, you must protect the worksheet *after* you've hidden data. To do so, Choose Tools ➤ Protection ➤ Protect Sheet. Assign a password if you like, and specify what should be hidden. When you are finished, click OK. To unprotect the sheet, choose Tools ➤ Protection ➤ Unprotect Sheet.

To hide a row or column:

1 Place the cursor in the row or column you wish to hide.

2 Choose either Format ➤ Row ➤ Hide or Format ➤ Column ➤ Hide. Alternatively, move the pointer to the bottom of the number heading (for rows) or the left of the letter heading (for columns) and then click and drag until the row or column is no longer visible.

3 To unhide hidden rows or columns, choose either Format ➤ Row ➤ Unhide or Format ➤ Column ➤ Unhide.

Do not confuse hiding rows and columns with deleting them (discussed in the "Delete" entry). Deleting them gets rid of them permanently; hiding them just puts them out of sight.

See Also   Columns, Delete, Protecting Worksheets, Rows

INSERT

The most common use of the *Insert* commands is to create additional cells in the middle of an already-made worksheet. Other commands on the Insert menu are covered in the sections that explain them fully.

To insert a column or row:

1 Click in the cell where you would like the new cells to go.

From here you have two choices, the automatic way or the manual way. To let Excel do things automatically, go on to step 2. To have more control, skip to step 3.

2 Choose either Insert ➤ Column or Insert ➤ Row. Note that inserted rows go above the highlighted cell, while inserted columns go to the left of it. Excel will place the new row or column. You can skip the remaining steps in this list.

3 Choose Insert ➤ Cells to bring up the Insert dialog box:

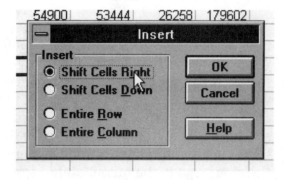

Notice that here you can add individual cells. The automatic method allows you to add whole columns or rows only.

4 Choose whether you want to place individual cells or entire rows or columns.

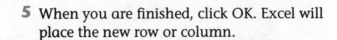

5 When you are finished, click OK. Excel will
place the new row or column.

To insert more than one column or row, choose more than
one cell before giving one of the Insert commands. For
example, if you want to insert three rows, choose three
cells (stacked vertically), and then choose Insert ➤ Rows.
Excel will add three new rows to your worksheet.

See Also Charts, Delete, Functions, Macros, Names, Page
Breaks

KEYBOARD SHORTCUTS

Quite a few of the menu commands and functions in Excel
have *keyboard shortcuts* (sometimes called *shortcut combinations*).
A keyboard shortcut is a combination of several keys that gives
the command; occasionally a shortcut will involve only one key,
which is usually a *function key,* one of the keys labeled F1–F15
along the top of your keyboard. The rationale behind keyboard
shortcuts is that it they make it easier to give commands right
from the keyboard as you work, rather than having to reach for
the mouse, go to the menu, and choose the command.

Table 3.1 lists Excel's keyboard shortcuts along with the commands and functions they execute.

Table 3.1	KEY	ACTION/COMMAND
Keyboard Shortcuts	**Changes from Excel 4**	
	F4	Repeat last action
	F7	Check spelling
	Ctrl+F	Find
	Ctrl+H	Replace
	Shift+F4	Find next
	Ctrl+Shift+F4	Find previous
	Ctrl+N	Open new workbook
	Ctrl+O	Open
	Ctrl+S	Save
	Ctrl+P	Print
	Ctrl+Tab	Next window
	Ctrl+Shift+Tab	Previous window
	Ctrl+PgDn	Move to next sheet in workbook
	Ctrl+PgUp	Move to previous sheet in workbook
	Ctrl+A	Select all
	Entering and Editing	
	F2	Edit active cell
	Esc	Cancel entry
	Backspace	Delete character to left of insertion point, or delete selection
	Shift+F2	Edit cell note
	F3	Paste name into formula
	Shift+F3	Display Function Wizard

Table 3.1	KEY	ACTION/COMMAND
Keyboard Shortcuts (continued)	Ctrl+A	After typing valid function name in formula, display step 2 of Function Wizard
	Ctrl+Shift+A	After typing valid function name in formula, insert argument names for the function
	Alt+=	Insert AutoSum formula
	Ctrl+semicolon	Enter date in cell or formula bar
	Ctrl+Shift+colon	Enter time in cell or formula bar
	Ctrl+D	Fill down
	Ctrl+R	Fill right
	Ctrl+Del	Cut text to end of line
	Alt+↵	Insert carriage return
	Ctrl+Alt+Tab	Insert tab
	Arrow keys	Move one character up, down, left, or right
	Ctrl+Shift+"	Copy value from cell above the active cell
	Ctrl+' (single left quotation mark)	Alternate between displaying values or formulas
	Ctrl+' (apostrophe)	Copy formula from cell above the active cell
	Ctrl+↵	Fill a selection of cells with current entry
	Ctrl+Shift+↵	Enter array formula
	F4	Change cell reference type (absolute-relative-mixed)

Table 3.1	KEY	ACTION/COMMAND
Keyboard Shortcuts (continued)	**Command Keys**	
	Ctrl+N	New workbook
	Ctrl+O	Open
	Ctrl+S	Save
	F12	Save As
	Ctrl+P	Print
	Alt+F4	Close Excel
	Ctrl+Z (or Alt+Backspace)	Undo
	F4	Repeat
	Ctrl+X	Cut
	Ctrl+C	Copy
	Ctrl+V	Paste
	Ctrl+D	Fill down
	Ctrl+R	Fill right
	Del	Clear contents (in worksheet); clear selected item (in chart)
	Ctrl+F	Display Find dialog box
	Ctrl+H	Display Replace dialog box
	Shift+F4	Find next
	Ctrl+Shift+F4	Find previous
	F5	Go To
	Ctrl+minus sign	Delete selected cells
	Ctrl+Shift+plus sign	Display Insert dialog box
	Shift+F11	Insert new worksheet
	F11	Insert new chart sheet
	Ctrl+F11	Insert new Excel 4.0 macro sheet

Table 3.1	KEY	ACTION/COMMAND
Keyboard Shortcuts (continued)	Ctrl+F3	Display Define Name dialog box
	F3	Display Paste Name dialog box (if names are defined)
	Ctrl+Shift+F3	Display Create Names dialog box
	Ctrl+1	Display Format Cells dialog box
	Ctrl+9	Hide rows
	Ctrl+Shift+(	Unhide rows
	Ctrl+0 (zero)	Hide columns
	Ctrl+Shift+)	Unhide columns
	Alt+' (apostrophe)	Display Style dialog box
	F7	Check spelling
	Ctrl+F6	Next window
	Ctrl+Shift+F6	Previous window
	F6	Next pane
	Shift+F6	Previous pane
	F1	Help Contents screen
	Ctrl+7	Show or hide Standard toolbar
	F9 or Ctrl+=	Calculate all open workbooks
	Shift+F9	Calculate active sheet

Function Keys

	F1	Help Contents screen
	Shift+F1	Display help pointer
	F2	Activate formula bar
	Shift+F2	Insert note
	Ctrl+F2	Display Info window
	F3	Display Paste Name dialog box (if names are defined)

Table 3.1	KEY	ACTION/COMMAND
Keyboard Shortcuts (continued)	Shift+F3	Display Function Wizard
	Ctrl+F3	Display Define Name dialog box
	Ctrl+Shift+F3	Display Create Names dialog box
	F4	When editing a formula, change cell reference type (absolute-relative-mixed); when not editing a formula, repeat last action
	Ctrl+F4	Close window
	Alt+F4	Close Excel
	F5	Go To
	Ctrl+F5	Restore window size
	F6	Next pane
	Shift+F6	Previous pane
	Ctrl+F6	Next window
	Ctrl+Shift+F6	Previous window
	F7	Check spelling
	Ctrl+F7	Move command (document Control menu)
	F8	Turn Extend mode on or off
	Shift+F8	Turn Add mode on or off
	Ctrl+F8	Size command (document Control menu)
	F9	Calculate all sheets in all open workbooks
	Shift+F9	Calculate active sheet
	Ctrl+F9	Minimize workbook
	F10	Activate menu bar
	Shift+F10	Activate shortcut menu

Table 3.1	KEY	ACTION/COMMAND
Keyboard Shortcuts (continued)	Ctrl+F10	Maximize workbook
	F11	Insert new chart sheet
	Shift+F11	Insert new worksheet
	Ctrl+F11	Insert new Excel 4.0 macro sheet
	F12	Save As
	Shift+F12	Save
	Ctrl+F12	Open
	Ctrl+Shift+F12	Print

Moving and Selecting in Worksheets and Workbooks

↵	Move down through selected cells
Shift+↵	Move up through selection
Tab	Move right through selection; move among unlocked cells in protected worksheet
Shift+Tab	Move left through selection
Ctrl+Backspace	Scroll to display active cell
Arrow key	Move by one cell in direction of arrow
Shift+*arrow key*	Extend selection by one cell
Ctrl+↑ or Ctrl+↓	Move up or down to edge of current data region
Ctrl+← or Ctrl+→	Move left or right to edge of current data region
Ctrl+Shift+*arrow key*	Extend selection to edge of current data region (in direction of arrow)
Home	Move to beginning of row
Shift+Home	Extend selection to beginning of row
Ctrl+Home	Move to beginning of worksheet

Table 3.1	KEY	ACTION/COMMAND
Keyboard Shortcuts (continued)	Ctrl+Shift+Home	Extend selection to beginning of worksheet
	Ctrl+End	Move to last cell in worksheet (lower-right corner)
	Ctrl+Shift+End	Extend selection to last cell in worksheet (lower-right corner)
	Ctrl+spacebar	Select entire column
	Shift+spacebar	Select entire row
	Ctrl+A	Select entire worksheet
	Shift+Backspace	Collapse selection to active cell
	PgDn	Move down one screen
	PgUp	Move up one screen
	Alt+PgDn	Move right one screen
	Alt+PgUp	Move left one screen
	Ctrl+PgDn	Move to next sheet in workbook
	Ctrl+PgUp	Move to previous sheet in workbook
	Shift+PgDn	Extend selection down one screen
	Shift+PgUp	Extend selection up one screen
	Ctrl+Shift+*	Select current region
	Ctrl+Shift+spacebar	When an object is selected, select all objects on sheet
	Ctrl+6	Alternate between hiding objects, displaying objects, and displaying placeholders for objects

Moving and Selecting While in End Mode

End	Turn End mode on/off
End, *arrow key*	Move by one block of data within a row or column

Table 3.1	KEY	ACTION/COMMAND
Keyboard Shortcuts (continued)	End, Shift+*arrow key*	Extend selection to end of data block in direction of arrow
	End, Home	Move to last cell in worksheet (lower-right corner)
	End, Shift+Home	Extend selection to last cell in worksheet (lower-right corner)
	End, ↵	Move to last cell in current row
	End, Shift+↵	Extend selection to last cell in current row

Moving and Selecting with Scroll Lock On

Scroll Lock	Turn scroll lock on/off
↑ or ↓	Scroll screen up or down one row
← or →	Scroll screen left or right one column
Home	Move to upper-left cell in window
End	Move to lower-right cell in window
Shift+Home	Extend selection to upper-left cell in window
Shift+End	Extend selection to lower-right cell in window

Selecting Special Cells

Ctrl+Shift+?	Select all cells containing a note
Ctrl+Shift+*	Select rectangular range of cells around the active cell—range selected is an area enclosed by any combination of blank rows and blank columns
Ctrl+/	Select entire array, if any, to which active cell belongs

Table 3.1	KEY	ACTION/COMMAND
Keyboard Shortcuts (continued)	Ctrl+\	Select cells whose contents are different from the comparison cell in each row
	Ctrl+Shift+¦	Select cells whose contents are different from the comparison cell in each column
	Ctrl+[	Select only cells directly referred to by formulas in selection
	Ctrl+Shift+{	Select all cells directly or indirectly referred to by formulas in selection
	Ctrl+]	Select only cells with formulas that refer directly to active cell
	Ctrl+Shift+}	Select all cells within formulas that directly or indirectly refer to active cell
	Alt+semicolon	Select only visible cells in current selection

Formatting

	Alt+' (apostrophe)	Display Style dialog box
	Ctrl+Shift+~	General number format
	Ctrl+Shift+$	Currency format with two decimal places (negative numbers appear in parentheses)
	Ctrl+Shift+%	Percentage format with no decimal places
	Ctrl+Shift+^	Exponential number format with two decimal places
	Ctrl+Shift+#	Date format with day, month, and year
	Ctrl+Shift+@	Time format with hour and minute (indicate a.m. or p.m.)

Table 3.1	KEY	ACTION/COMMAND
Keyboard Shortcuts (continued)	Ctrl+Shift+!	Two-decimal-place format with commas
	Ctrl+Shift+&	Apply outline border
	Ctrl+Shift+_	Remove all borders
	Ctrl+B	Apply or remove bold (toggle)
	Ctrl+I	Apply or remove italic (toggle)
	Ctrl+U	Apply or remove underline (toggle)
	Ctrl+5	Apply or remove strikethrough (toggle)
	Ctrl+9	Hide rows
	Ctrl+Shift+(	Unhide rows
	Ctrl+0 (zero)	Hide columns
	Ctrl+Shift+)	Unhide columns

Outlining

	Alt+Shift+←	Ungroup a row or column
	Alt+Shift+→	Group a row or column
	Ctrl+8	Display or hide outline symbols
	Ctrl+9	Hide selected rows
	Ctrl+Shift+(	Unhide selected rows
	Ctrl+0 (zero)	Hide selected columns
	Ctrl+Shift+)	Unhide selected columns

Print Preview Mode

	Arrow keys	Move around page when zoomed in
	↑, ↓	Move by one page when zoomed out
	PgUp, PgDn	Move by one page when zoomed out; move around page when zoomed in

Table 3.1	KEY	ACTION/COMMAND
Keyboard Shortcuts (continued)	Ctrl+↑ or Ctrl+←	Move to first page when zoomed out
	Ctrl+↓ or Ctrl+→	Move to last page when zoomed out

Selecting Chart Items When Chart Is Active

↓	Select previous group of items
↑	Select next group of items
→	Select next item within group
←	Select previous item within group

Using AutoFilter

Alt+↓	Display drop-down list for selected column label
Alt+↑	Close drop-down list for selected column label
↑	Select previous item in list
↓	Select next item in list
Home	Select first item in list (All)
End	Select last item in list (NonBlanks)
↵	Filter worksheet list using selected item

Window Commands

Ctrl+F4	Close window
Ctrl+F5	Restore window size
Ctrl+F6 or Ctrl+Tab	Next window
Ctrl+Shift+F6 or Ctrl+Shift+Tab	Previous window
Ctrl+F7	Move command (Control menu)
Ctrl+F8	Size command (Control menu)

Table 3.1	KEY	ACTION/COMMAND
Keyboard	Ctrl+F9	Minimize window
Shortcuts	Ctrl+F10	Maximize window
(continued)	**Switching Applications**	
	Alt+Esc	Next application
	Alt+Shift+Esc	Previous application
	Alt+Tab	Next Windows application
	Alt+Shift+Tab	Previous Windows application
	Ctrl+Esc	Display Task List dialog box

Note: for keyboards with only ten function keys, use Alt+F1 for F11; use Alt+F2 for F12.

LABELS

Labels are useful to have in charts. Usually used in bar charts, a label goes next to a bar in the chart and notes the exact amount the bar is supposed to represent. This can be handy if it's not perfectly clear what the actual number is that the bar stands for (which is often the case).

To add labels to a chart:

1 Double-click the chart to make it active.

2 Choose Insert ➤ Data Labels. The Data Labels dialog box appears:

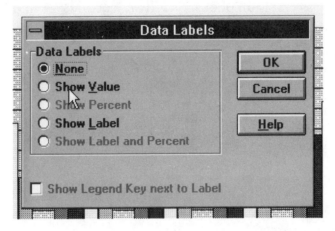

3 The default is None. To place labels on the chart:

- ✔ Click on Show Value to place the values above the bars.
- ✔ Click Show Label to use the labels shown along the x axis instead.

4 Click OK to have Excel add the labels.

Too many data labels can make a chart quite cluttered, so use labels with discretion. After you place the labels on a chart, look at the chart to see how easy the labels are to read. The purpose of labels is to make a chart more useful.

See Also Charts, ChartWizard

LEGEND

A *legend* is a list in a chart that helps explain what the data is all about. Usually a legend is set in a box off to one side of the chart, and it shows what the amounts indicate, like so:

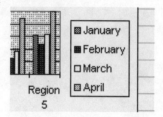

To add a legend to a chart that doesn't have one, use one of these techniques:

- Click on the chart to select it, and click the Legend button on the Chart toolbar.

- Double-click to activate the chart and choose Insert ➤ Legend. Excel will add the legend.

See Also   Axis Labels, Chart Toolbar, Charts, ChartWizard

LINKS

By using *links,* you can avoid a lot of duplicate effort, as well as ensure accuracy among workbooks that rely on common information. A link is essentially a piece of data copied from one workbook and pasted into another with a connection between the two. After the link is made, if you change the original piece of data (called the *source*), the linked data in the other workbook (the *destination* workbook) will be updated. You decide whether updating is automatic or manual.

To establish a link between two workbooks:

1 In the source workbook, copy the piece of data you wish to have linked in other workbooks. To do this, select the data and click the Copy button in the Standard toolbar.

2 Go to the destination workbook and click where you want the linked data to go.

3 Choose Edit ➤ Paste Special. The Paste Special dialog box appears:

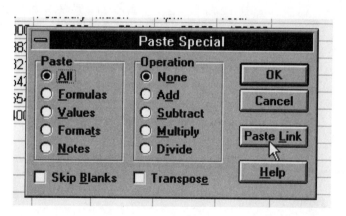

4 Click on Paste Link. Excel will establish the link between the two workbooks.

From now on, whenever you open the source document, Excel will ask if you want to update links. Click yes to do so. To make link updating automatic:

1 Go to the destination workbook.

2 Choose Edit ➤ Links. The Links dialog box appears:

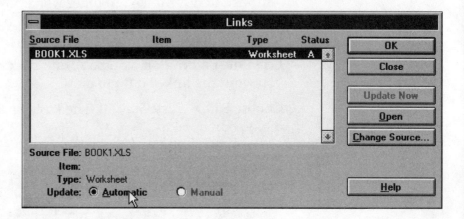

3 Choose the Automatic option next to Update and click OK.

See Also   Automatic Update; Cut, Copy, and Paste

MACROS

Perhaps one of the most useful features of Excel is its *macro* utility. And it's so easy to use! A macro is nothing more than a sequence of commands and actions. You can assign a macro a name and place it in a menu, or you can assign it to a button on a toolbar. Then, you can execute the macro by clicking the button or choosing the menu command. If you do a lot of repetitive or complicated command sequences, assign them to macros—it'll speed up your work!

Let's try recording and playing back a macro. Since there is no quick command for freezing panes, let's write a macro that freezes panes, and then make a shortcut combination for it.

1 Split your worksheet into two panes. To do this, choose Window ➤ Split.

2 Choose View ➤ Toolbars. The Toolbars dialog box appears:

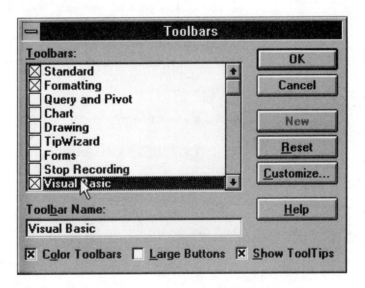

3 The macro toolbar is called Visual Basic (after the Visual Basic computer language). Click to place an *X* next to Visual Basic and click OK. The Visual Basic toolbar appears on your spreadsheet.

4 Click the Record Macro button on the Visual Basic toolbar. A dialog box appears asking you to name the macro.

5 Name it **FreezePanes**. When you've typed the name, click OK.

A message appears in the status bar saying that the macro is recording.

6 Choose Window ➤ Freeze Panes.

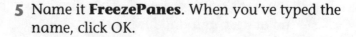

7 Click the Stop Macro button on the Visual Basic toolbar. The macro will stop recording. You can tell recording has stopped because the word *Ready* appears in the status bar.

8 Before going on, choose Window ➤ Unfreeze Panes.

Now let's test the macro:

1 Click the Run Macro button on the Visual Basic toolbar.

2 In the Macro dialog box, select FreezePanes and click on the Run button. The macro freezes the top pane of the split window.

Now let's make a shortcut key for our macro:

1 Click the Run Macro button on the Visual Basic toolbar. The Macro dialog box comes up again.

2 Select FreezePanes and click on the Options button.

Since the command is already on a menu, let's just assign a shortcut key:

3 Click the Shortcut Key option and enter a key next to the word *Ctrl+*. Then select Close.

Whenever you press Ctrl+ your new shortcut key, it will freeze the top pane of a split window.

See Also   Freezing Panes, Splitting Windows

MARGINS

A *margin* is the white space that appears between the edge of the page and your data when it is printed. There are four margins: top, bottom, left, and right. You might adjust margins for a number of reasons, but the most common is to make the print area larger to get more information on the page.

To change margins:

1   Choose File ➤ Page Setup. The Page Setup dialog box appears:

2 Click the Margins tab to bring it to the front.

3 Adjust the worksheet's margins as necessary by typing in new settings in the Top, Bottom, Left, and Right boxes. You can see your changes in the preview area.

4 When you are finished, click OK to put your new margins into effect.

See Also Page Breaks, Page Setup

Markers

A *data marker* is a symbol in a chart that represents a single value. You might use data markers to indicate how a series of values relate to one another. This is called a *data series*.

To create a data series in a chart:

1 Double-click to activate the chart.

2 Decide which values you would like to highlight, and double-click on one of them. The Format Data Series dialog box appears.

There are five tabs in this dialog box for specifying patterns, axes, name and values, y error bars, and data labels.

3 Click each tab to bring it forward and make your changes.

4 When you are finished, click OK.

See Also Charts, ChartWizard

MENUS

As you've no doubt noticed, nine names appear in the *menu bar* across the top of the screen. If you click on one of these menu names, you will see one of Excel's nine *menus*. Each menu has a number of related commands. To choose a command, click the menu's name, slide down to the desired command, and click on it. The command will then execute.

An alternate way to give menu commands is to press Alt, then the underlined letter in the menu's name (for example, *o* in the Format menu), then the underlined letter in the command (for example, *e* for the Cells command).

Excel's menus are organized as follows:

File Offers commands for file management, such as Save and Open, along with the printing commands.

Edit Offers commands for cutting, copying, and pasting information within and between worksheets, as well as the Find, Replace, and Go To commands.

View Offers commands for controlling the appearance of the screen, including the toolbars, status bar, and formula bar, as well as the Zoom command.

Insert Offers commands for placing objects in worksheets, such as rows, columns, pictures, and functions, as well as the Name command.

Format Offers commands for formatting various parts of your worksheets. The AutoFormat command is available here.

Tools A catch-all menu, it offers a variety of useful utilities, including the spelling checker, the auditing utility, the macro commands, and the Options command, which allows you to customize Excel to your liking.

Data Offers commands for manipulating the data in spreadsheets, including sorts, forms, tables, and PivotTables.

Window Lists all open workbooks and offers commands for manipulating windows.

Help Offers commands related to the Help facility.

See Also   Recently Used Workbook Files, Shortcut Menus

MOVING BETWEEN WORKSHEETS

At times you want to see data that is on a worksheet other than the one showing. Moving between worksheets is a breeze:

✔ Simply click the sheet tab you wish to go to. Excel will bring that sheet forward:

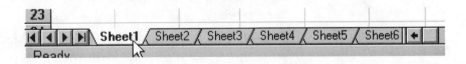

There are also a few shortcuts worth knowing about. You can click on the tab scrolling buttons as follows:

⊳ Click this button to scroll to the first tab in the worksheet.

⊳ Click this button to scroll to the previous tab in the worksheet.

⊳ Click this button to scroll to the next tab in the worksheet.

⊳ Click this button to scroll to the last tab in the worksheet.

See Also   Multiple Worksheets, Sheet Tabs

MULTIPLE WORKSHEETS

All Excel workbooks are divided into *worksheets*. By default, new workbooks have 16 worksheets. By interconnecting worksheets, you can have three-dimensional workbooks. This means you can, for instance, keep track of how much profit (first dimension) was made during specific periods (second dimension) on certain products (third dimension). This is a very sophisticated way of tracking, but it is quite easy with Excel. With multiple worksheets, you can do some pretty amazing things, such as summing values across worksheets and placing the totals on yet another worksheet. Take a moment to imagine other scenarios where 3-D workbooks would be useful. (Don't fall asleep now!)

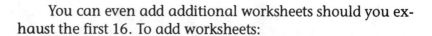

You can even add additional worksheets should you exhaust the first 16. To add worksheets:

1 Click on the tab of the worksheet you want a new worksheet inserted *in front of*.

2 Choose Insert ➤ Worksheet. The new worksheet will be added where you have specified:

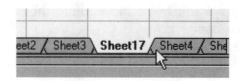

See Also 3D Ranges, Moving between Worksheets, Splitting Windows

NAMES

You can assign *names* to cells or ranges in your worksheet. Naming regions is an excellent idea, because you can reference them in formulas *by name,* which saves you from having to remember where they are. Other actions can be carried out on named regions, speeding up your work. For example, you can type names in the Go To box to go directly to them. This is very handy for moving around large spreadsheets.

To assign a name to a region:

1 Select the cell or range you wish to name.

2 Choose Insert ➤ Name ➤ Define to bring up the
   Define Name dialog box:

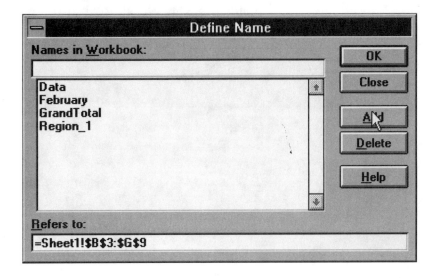

   If you have chosen a range that has a title, Excel may automatically insert the title into the Names in Workbook box.

3 Either accept the suggested name or type in one
   of your own.

4 Click OK to create the named region.

See Also 3D Ranges, Formula Bar, Ranges

Nᴇᴡ

   When you want to work with a clean, unsullied workbook,
one that is chaste and pure, pure as the driven snow, untouched

by the hand of man…well, you get the idea, you must open a *new* workbook. To do so, use one of these techniques:

- ✔ Click the New Workbook button on the Standard toolbar
- ✔ Choose File ➤ New
- ✔ Press Ctrl+N

> By default, new workbooks open with 16 worksheets. Also, new workbooks take on whatever attributes you set in the Options dialog box, reached with Tools ➤ Options. Each time you open a new workbook, its name is Book*n*, where *n* is the number of new workbooks you have opened this session.

See Also   Open

NUMBERING PAGES

See Page Numbering.

OBJECT LINKING AND EMBEDDING

Object Linking and Embedding is beyond the scope of this book. Consult Excel's help system for information.

OPEN

When you want a completely clean, new workbook, you use the File ➤ New command. But what about accessing workbooks you've already worked on, perhaps to revise information? Then you use the Open command.

To open a workbook, use one of these techniques to bring up the Open dialog box:

✔ Click the Open button on the Standard toolbar

✔ Choose File ➤ Open

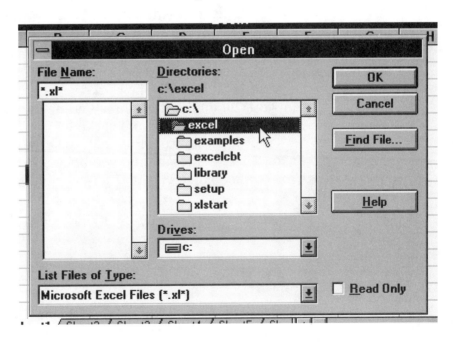

In the Open dialog box, notice that Excel has already added *.xl* in the File Name box. This tells the open function to list all files with the .xl* extension—that is, Excel files. If you want to open other types of files, either type *.* and click OK or open the List Files of Type drop-down list, click on the type of file you want, and then double-click on it in the File Name box.

2 Click on the file you want to open. If you don't see it listed, click on various folders in the Directories list to see their contents, and when you find the file you want to open, click on it.

3 Click OK.

Excel will open up the workbook you have chosen. Note that you can double-click a file's name in step 2 above to open it instead of clicking on it and clicking OK.

You might notice names of files at the bottom of the File menu. These are recent files you have opened. See the "Recently Used Workbook Files" entry for full details.

See Also   New, Recently Used Workbook Files, Starting Excel

PAGE BREAKS

Excel does not always choose the best ways to lay out your data on the printed page. Fortunately, you have a lot of control over how printed worksheets look. For example, you can widen the margins to fit more information on a page. Also, you can specify where Excel should start a new page by inserting manual *page breaks*.

To insert page breaks:

1 Place the cursor in the cell where you want the page breaks to go. Excel will place the breaks just *above* and to the *left* of the chosen cell.

2 Choose Insert ➤ Page Break. Excel will place the break:

B	C	D	E	F	G	H
anuary	February	March	April	Total		
45000	54900	53444	26258	179602		
26383	62638	26275	37354	152650		
45821	44114	45458	74154	209547		
52542	25852	36524	89547	204465		
62654	46957	63636	99522	272769		
232400	234461	225337	326835	1019033		

To get rid of a manual break, go to the cell you chose before and choose Insert ➤ Remove Page Break.

See Also Margins, Print

PAGE NUMBERING

It is always a good idea to *number* the pages of printed worksheets. Then, if the worksheet is several pages long, people reading it will know if a page is missing. You specify page numbers in the Page Setup dialog box.

To set page numbers:

1 Choose File ➤ Page Setup. The Page Setup dialog box appears:

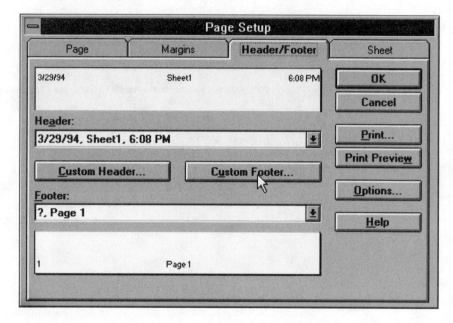

2 Click the Header/Footer Sheet to bring it forward.

3 Click on either the Custom Header or Custom Footer button. Usually page numbers go at the bottom of the page. Either the Header or the Footer dialog box appears.

4 Click in the Section area (Left, Center, or Right) where you want the page number to go.

 5 Click the Page Number button. Excel will insert the function for page numbers (&[Page]).

6 You can type text into the Section boxes, and it will appear on the printed page. One nice use of this feature is to insert a page number, as we did in Step 5, then type the word *of* and click the Total Pages button.

Excel will insert the function for total number of pages (&[Pages]). Then, on every page, Excel will print something like *3 of 12* to inform readers where they are in the worksheet. This can be especially handy for very large worksheets.

7 When you are finished, click OK several times to close the dialog boxes.

See Also Headers and Footers, Page Setup

PAGE SETUP

The *Page Setup* command gives you a lot of control over the printed appearance of worksheets. Margins, page numbering, and headers and footers are all covered in depth elsewhere in this reference, so let's concentrate on the other two areas of interest, Page and Sheet.

To adjust the page setup of your worksheet:

1 Choose File ➤ Page Setup. The Page Setup Dialog box appears:

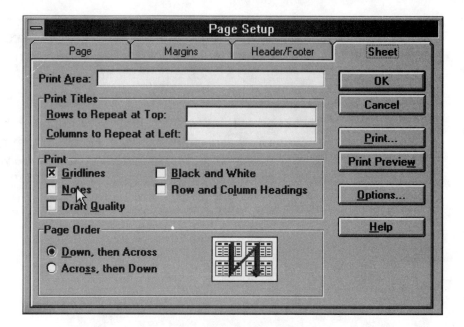

2 Click on the various tabs to bring them forward (see below), and when you are done click OK.

As mentioned above, the Margins and Header/Footer tabs are covered elsewhere in detail. The Page tab is where you control the following:

Orientation Controls whether your worksheet prints vertically or horizontally on the page. Landscape (horizontal) is best for wide worksheets that are not very tall. Portrait (vertical) is best for tall worksheets that are not wide. If you have a worksheet that is both tall and wide, either put it on a diet or visit a Big & Tall shop.

Scaling Controls how large the worksheet should print. Setting the percentage to 50, for instance, prints the worksheet at half its normal size.

You can even instruct Excel to fit the worksheet's data in a finite number of pages.

Paper Size   Specifies the physical size of the paper you'll be printing to.

Print Quality   Allows you to print "draft" copies of your worksheets (for proofing, perhaps) at 150 dpi (medium quality) or even 75 dpi (low quality). This should be set to 300 for final output.

First Page Number   Allows you to start numbering worksheet pages from a number other than 1 (Auto).

Click on the Sheet tab to control the following:

Print Area   Allows you to specify a certain range of data to print. This way you can print out just what you want, without having to print the whole worksheet.

Print Titles   Allows you to print the rows and columns that contain titles on every page for ease of reading.

Print   Allows you to specify whether certain items print along with data. These include gridlines, notes, and row and column headings.

Page Order   Tells Excel what order to print your worksheets in.

See Also   Headers and Footers, Margins, Page Numbering, Print

PANES

See Freezing Panes, Splitting Windows.

PASTE

See Cut, Copy, and Paste.

PATTERNS

See Borders and Shading.

PRINT

Printing is pretty straightforward in Excel. To print a document:

1 Begin by using one of these techniques:

✔ Click the Print button on the Standard toolbar. Using this technique, Excel sends the document straight to the printer, bypassing the Print dialog box.

✔ Choose File ➤ Print to see the Print dialog box.

✔ Press Ctrl+P to see the Print dialog box.

It is always a good idea to check your worksheet's page setup before printing. To do so, choose File ➤ Page Setup. Here you can check your margins, headers/footers, etc. It is also wise to visit Print Preview before printing. This way, you can catch and fix minor problems before you waste any paper.

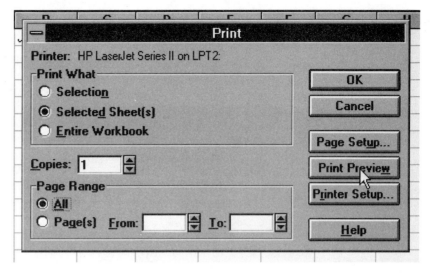

2 Adjust the settings in the Print dialog box to your liking.

You can print more than one copy, or you can print just a section of the worksheet. Also, you can click the Page Setup or Print Preview buttons to bring up those dialog boxes.

3 When you are satisfied with the settings, click OK.

See Also Margins, Page Numbering, Page Setup, Print Preview

PRINT PREVIEW

Print Preview is the world's greatest paper saver! It saves trees, time, and tempers. The importance of this command cannot be overemphasized. It allows you to see more or less exactly how your document will look on the printed page. Here is where

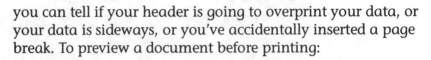

you can tell if your header is going to overprint your data, or your data is sideways, or you've accidentally inserted a page break. To preview a document before printing:

1 Use one of these techniques to see the Print Preview screen:

> ✔ Click the Print Preview button on the Standard toolbar
> ✔ Choose File ➤ Print Preview

2 Use these techniques to examine the document:

> ✔ Double-click on the document or click the Zoom button to get in close.
> ✔ Click the Setup button to visit the Page Setup dialog box.
> ✔ Click Margins to show the margins. You can even adjust them by clicking and dragging!

3 If you're not ready to print, click Close to return to your worksheet. If you are ready, click Print, and the Print dialog box will appear, where it's business as usual.

> ***See Also***   Headers and Footers, Page Setup, Print

PROTECTING WORKSHEETS

To prevent the data in worksheets from being changed, you *protect* them. Sometimes, protecting worksheets is the only safeguard against idiots. It is important to specify cells as either hidden or locked *before* you turn protection on. See the "Hide" entry.

To protect a worksheet:

1 Choose Tools ➤ Protection ➤ Protect Sheet. The Protect Sheet dialog box appears:

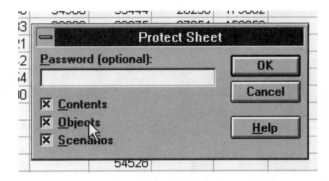

2 Click to check or uncheck the options boxes, depending on the level of protection you want.

3 Add a password if you don't want other users to unprotect your worksheet.

4 When you are satisfied with the settings, click OK.

To unprotect the worksheet, choose Tools ➤ Protection ➤ Unprotect. If you assigned a password, you'll have to provide it before Excel will remove protection.

It is important to know how to protect your worksheet, because hiding and locking cells has no effect unless the worksheet is protected. The distinction between *locked* and *hidden* is that, in a locked cell, the data cannot be edited, whereas in a hidden cell, any formula information is hidden from the user.

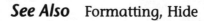

See Also   Formatting, Hide

QUITTING EXCEL

See Exiting Excel.

RANGES

A *range* is a collection of adjacent cells. Ranges can include

- Single cells
- Several adjacent cells
- Adjacent sets of cells over several worksheets
- Entire rows
- Entire columns
- Entire worksheets
- Entire workbooks

The concept of ranges is very important in formulas, because a range can serve as a shorthand method for writing out cells you want to manipulate. For instance, if you wanted to sum a column of numbers, instead of typing

    =sum(B2+B3+B4+B5+B6)

you could type

    =sum(B2:B6)

into the formula bar. In this example, *B2:B6* is a range.

You separate the arguments in a range with a colon (:) if they are on the same worksheet. If you want to specify a range on a different worksheet, you must include the name of the worksheet, along with an exclamation point (!).

Another very useful property of ranges is that you can name them. Then, when you want to use the range in a formula, you can just type its name instead. Yet another advantage of named ranges is that you can go directly to them in the Go To dialog box.

See Also   3D Ranges, Formulas, Names

RECALCULATION

When you change the value of a cell that is included in a formula, the formula updates the information in its own cell instantaneously. In other words, if you have a sum formula and you change one of the cells being summed, the result of the formula is *recalculated* automatically.

There may be times, however, when automatic recalculation is a bad idea. For example, if you had a humongous worksheet with hundreds of complex formulas and you recalculated them, you might have to wait a long time to find out the results. You can turn off automatic recalculation and have the program recalculate only when you press F9.

To turn off automatic recalculation:

1 Select Tools ➤ Options to bring up the Options dialog box.

2 Click on the Calculation tab to bring it forward.

In the upper-left corner is the Calculation area:

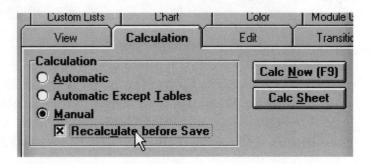

3 Click Manual to turn off automatic recalculation.

If you like, you can have Excel do a recalculation even if you don't tell it to before saving by activating the Recalculation before Save box. This way, you can recalculate only when you save a worksheet and save yourself the trouble of having to wait for recalculations to occur.

4 When you are finished, click OK.

Now, when you want to do a recalculation, you press F9— the special key!

See Also Save

RECENTLY USED WORKBOOK FILES

Sort of a shortcut version of the Open command, the list of files at the bottom of the File menu shows the four most recently used files. To open a recently used file:

✔ Click the File menu and choose the file you want to open:

The last-four files feature is quite handy. But keep in mind that the last four files used will be listed *no matter what* they were, which can lead to a lot of embarrassment. If you don't want your boss to see that you have a work-sheet called *embezzle.xls*, you might want to disable this feature! To do so, uncheck the Recently Used File List option in the General tab of the Options dialog box (Tools ➤ Options).

See Also   Menus, Open

REDO

See Undo/Redo.

REPEAT

Repeat is a useful command under some circumstances, but much of its functionality can be accessed by way of other Excel commands, most notably by Format Painter. The command repeats the latest command or action. It resides on the Edit menu, and its name changes depending on what you've just done.

Perhaps the best use of the Repeat command is for redoing options you have chosen in dialog boxes. A good example is locking cells. The act of locking cells takes no fewer than five actions: clicking the Format menu, choosing Cells (Ctrl+1), clicking the Protection Tab, activating Locked, and clicking OK. Clearly, using the Repeat command is quicker and more efficient.

To repeat a command or action:

1 Use one of these techniques:

    ✔ Click the Repeat button on the Standard toolbar
    ✔ Choose Edit ➤ Repeat *action*
    ✔ Press F4

If an action or command cannot be repeated, the command will be dimmed and will display *Can't Repeat.*

See Also Format Painter, Undo/Redo

REPLACE

The Replace utility is a companion piece to the Find utility (discussed separately in the "Search" entry). Replace really just extends the functionality of Find. You can use Replace to change all kinds of elements in your worksheets, including text, numbers, and formulas. Common uses of this command are to replace instances of someone's name or to change all references to a range whose name or composition has changed.

Think carefully about what you want to replace with the Replace command. As you'll see, some actions cannot be undone!

To replace information:

1 Select a range if you want to limit the replace; otherwise, Excel will search the entire worksheet. To search multiple worksheets, select all the ones you want to perform the replace in.

2 Choose Edit ➤ Replace or press Ctrl+H. The Replace dialog box appears.

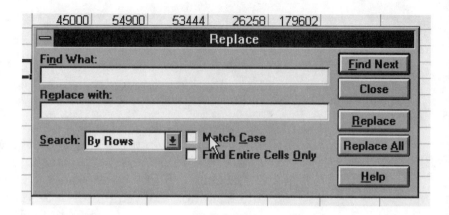

3 Type the text you wish to replace in the Find What box. For example, you might enter **B2:E9** if this range has now been extended to include other cells.

4 In the Replace With box, type what you want to replace the text in the Find What box. For example, you might want to replace our hypothetical range B2:E9 with **A2:F16**.

5 Click either Find Next or Replace All:

  ✔ **Replace All**   Replaces all instances of the Find What text. When the replacements have been made, the Replace dialog box closes.

  ✔ **Find Next**   Finds the first instance of the Find What text and highlights it. If you wish to replace it, click Replace; otherwise, click Find Next and Excel will find the next occurrence of the Find What text. When the worksheet or range has been searched in its entirety you will see a dialog box telling you that no more matching text exists. Click OK, then click Close.

If you want Excel to replace only those instances of the Find What text that *exactly* match the case of the original, click the Match Case option. Also, you can ensure that Excel replaces only instances of the original text that constitute entire cells by clicking the Find Entire Cells Only checkbox.

See Also   Search, Selecting

Rows

A *row* is a single horizontal array of cells. If you want to apply some kind of formatting to a row of data in a worksheet, it is usually a good idea to select the entire row. This way, if you later add *new* cells of data to the row, they will take on the formatting characteristics of the cells already in the row. See the "Selecting" entry for more details.

Changing Row Height

You can change the height of a row either automatically or manually. When you change row heights automatically, the entire height is adjusted to accommodate the tallest cell.

To change row heights automatically:

1 Select the row or rows. If you're just changing one row, you need only select one of its cells; however, if you want to change more than one row, you must select the *entire* row for all rows to be changed.

2 Position the cursor over the *bottom* border of the row's number heading. It will turn into a "plus" sign with arrows on the top and bottom.

3 Double-click. Excel automatically adjusts the row heights.

To change row heights manually:

1 Select the row or rows. If you're just changing one row, you need only select one of its cells; however, if you want to change more than one row, you must select the *entire* row for all rows to be changed.

2 Position the cursor over the *bottom* border of the row's number heading. It will turn into a "plus" sign with arrows on the top and bottom.

3 Click and hold the mouse button.

4 Move the pointer down to make the row shorter or up to make it taller. When you release the mouse button, the rows will adjust to their new height.

See Also Center across Columns, Columns, Selecting

SAVE

Perhaps the single most important command, Save is one that ensures you don't lose any data…at least not immediately. Any edits that you do to a worksheet that are not saved reside in a dark, mysterious, and volatile memory called *random access memory* (RAM). If for some reason Excel quits unexpectedly or your computer "hangs" on you (i.e., it doesn't respond to keyboard input, mouse movements, or swift kicks), any information that resides only in RAM will be lost irretrievably. The way to avoid this sort of tragedy is to save your work to the friendly and safe memory called *disk memory*. Put simply, save your work to disk early and often.

To save your work, use one of these techniques:

▱ Click the Save button on the Standard toolbar

▱ Choose File ➤ Save

▱ Press Ctrl+S

A very useful utility to know about is Tools ➤ *AutoSave*. You might not find it on your menus, though, because it is an associate program (also called an *add-in*) to Excel, and must be installed specially. It is in the Library directory, and might have been installed if you did the full installation of Excel.

See Also   Close, Converting Files to and from Excel, Exiting Excel, Save As

SAVE AS

To save a file under a new name or in a foreign file format:

1 Make sure the worksheet you want to save is the active one.

2 Choose File ➤ Save As. The Save As dialog box appears:

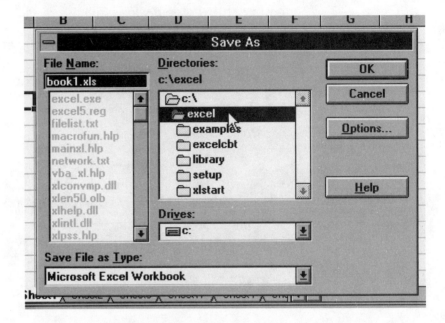

3 Type a new name for the file. If you want to save the new file in a different directory or to another disk, fiddle with the Directories and Drives lists until you've found the right location. If you want to save the file in standard Excel format (.xls), go on to step 6.

4 If you want to save the file in a foreign file format, click the down-arrow in the Save File as Type list and scroll until you find the format you want to translate the file into. Then click on the file format you want.

5 When you release the mouse button, the new format will appear in the Save File as Type box, and your file's extension will be changed to reflect the new format. Notice that Excel still gives the file the same name; it just changes the extension.

6 Click OK, and Excel will save the file under its new name in the format you have specified. If you have specified a format other than the standard Excel format, when you try to close the file you will get a message saying that the file is not in Excel format and asking if you want to save it as an Excel file. Just click No.

When you save an Excel file under a new name or in another format, you are not replacing the old file; rather, you are creating *another* file under a new name or in a new format. The file you are converting remains untouched on your hard disk.

See Also   Close, Converting Files to and from Excel, Exiting Excel, Save

SCROLL BARS

You use the *scroll bars* in Excel just as you use them in any Windows program. There are two scroll bars, the vertical and the

horizontal. The scroll bars are the gray shafts with the boxes inside them and the arrow buttons on either end:

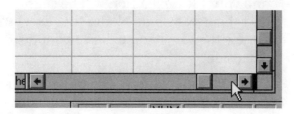

Scroll bars can be used in three different ways:

✔ Clicking in the gray part of the shaft scrolls an entire screen at a time.

✔ Clicking and dragging the boxes moves to specific areas of a worksheet.

✔ Clicking repeatedly or holding down the mouse button on the arrow buttons scrolls one row or one column at a time.

Scroll bars contain horizontal and vertical *split boxes*. You use these to manually split your worksheets into multiple windows. You can even freeze one of the panes, allowing you to scroll in the another while the data in the frozen one stays put. See the "Freezing Panes" and "Splitting Windows" entries.

See Also   Freezing Panes, Splitting Windows

SEARCH

You can search for text, numbers, and formulas by using the Find command, which is a sort of little brother of the Replace command. The Find command locates occurrences of specified character strings and highlights them for you.

To use the Find command:

1 Select a range if you want to limit the search; otherwise, Excel will search the entire worksheet. To search multiple worksheets, select all the ones you want to search in.

2 Choose Edit ➤ Find or press Ctrl+F. The Find dialog box appears:

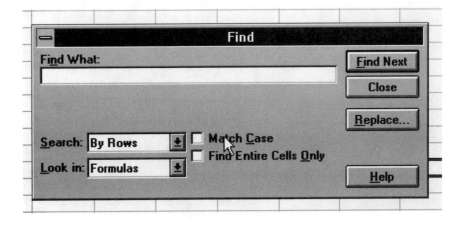

3 Type the text you wish to search for in the Find What box. For example, you might enter **B2:E9** if you wanted to examine all formulas that included this range.

4 Click Find Next.

Excel finds the first instance of the Find What text and high-lights it.

5 Click Find Next to find the next occurrence, or click Close to rid yourself of this wretched dialog box.

Note that you can click the Replace button in the Find dialog box to metamorphose it into the Replace dialog box. Replace is discussed in detail in the "Replace" entry.

See Also   Go To, Replace

SELECTING

Excel provides a variety of ways to *select* cells, ranges, and other objects. Following is a list of common mouse methods for selecting. This entry also explains selecting columns, rows, ranges, charts, and multiple worksheets.

To make selections with the mouse:

Clicking   Selects a single cell.

Click-dragging   Selects contiguous cells (cells right next to one another).

Shift-clicking   Also selects contiguous cells, but allows you to quickly select large ranges.

Ctrl-clicking   Selects noncontiguous cells (they don't have to be next to one another).

Use Shift in conjunction with ↑, ↓, →, ← to select one cell in the direction of the arrow; use Page Up or Page Down to select up or down one screen; use Home to select to the beginning of the row. There are numerous arrow and other key combinations that you can use to select cells.

To select an entire column:

1 Either position the pointer in the column you want to select and press Ctrl+spacebar, or move the pointer into the letter heading area of the column (the pointer will turn into a white "plus" sign):

A	B	C	D
	January	February	March

2 Click to select the column.

To select an entire row:

1 Either position the pointer in the row you want to select and press Shift+spacebar, or move the pointer into the number heading area of the row (the pointer will turn into a white "plus" sign):

5	Region 4	52542	
	Region 5	62654	
7		232400	2

2 Click to select the row.

To select a range:

1 Either Shift-drag or Shift-click on the cells you want to select. Alternately, you can use the Edit ➤ Go To command (F5) to bring up the Go To dialog box:

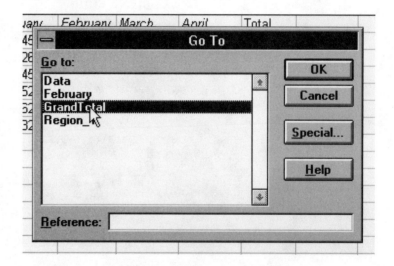

2 Double-click on the name of the range you want and it will be selected.

To select a chart:

✔ Simply double-click on it.

To select multiple worksheets:

1 Press Ctrl+A to select the first worksheet.

2 Click on other worksheets' tabs to visit them:

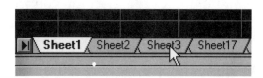

3 Press Ctrl+A to select all the cells in those worksheets.

4 Repeat steps 2 and 3 until all the worksheets you want to select are selected.

See Also Charts, Columns, Go To, Ranges, Rows

SHADING

See Borders and Shading.

SHEET TABS

In Excel, entire files are called *workbooks* (see the "Workbooks" entry). A workbook is a collection of worksheets, charts, and any other objects you have inserted, such as pictures. You move between the worksheets in a workbook by clicking *worksheet tabs,* which are usually called *sheet tabs.*

Moving between worksheets is a breeze:

🖉 Simply click the sheet tab you wish to go to. Excel will bring that sheet forward:

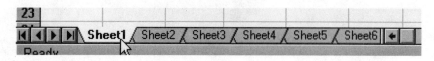

When you bring a sheet forward, you make it the *active* worksheet. Other worksheets may be *open* (loaded into memory), but only one worksheet can be active. The active worksheet is the only one you can work in. To use a different worksheet, you must first make it active. Similarly, only one workbook can be active at a time, though several can be open simultaneously.

Dialog box tabs work by the same principle as worksheet tabs. To access a particular tab, just click it. All tabs in a dialog box have OK, Cancel, and Help buttons:

OK   Click here after you have made settings on the tab and you want them to take effect.

Cancel   Click here when you decide you don't want to make any changes after all. Clicking Cancel leaves the dialog box.

Help   Click here to see a context-specific help screen about the tab you are in.

See Also Moving between Worksheets, Multiple Worksheets, Workbooks, Worksheets

SHORTCUT MENUS

At times it's inconvenient to use shortcut keys or choose commands from the menus. That's when *shortcut menus* come in handy. Generally speaking, any time you click the *right* mouse button (not the left), you get a shortcut menu. Shortcut menus vary, depending upon the immediate task at hand.

For example, if you are just editing along in a worksheet and click the right mouse button, this shortcut menu comes up:

May	June	July	August	Total
5000	549			79602
6383	626			52650
4528	441			18254
2542	258			04465
2654	469			72769
1107	2344			27740

> **Cut**
> **Copy**
> Paste
> Paste Special...
>
> **Insert...**
> **Delete...**
> **Clear Contents**
>
> **Format Cells...**

Here you can cut, copy, delete, clear, or format the selected cells. You can also insert cells if you wish. If you had cut or copied something before clicking the right mouse button, you would also see Paste options on the shortcut menu.

If you are in a chart instead of a worksheet and you click the right mouse button, this shortcut menu comes up:

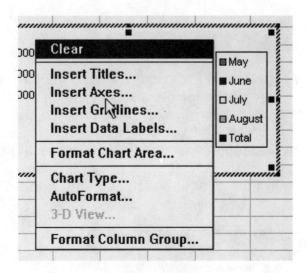

Here you can add titles, axes, gridlines, and labels, or change the chart type. You can even reach AutoFormat from here.

Regardless of which shortcut menu you use, they all work the same. You click the right mouse button to get the menu, and then just drag to or click on the command you want to execute, just like regular menus.

See Also   Menus

SORT

Excel allows you to *sort* information in variety of ways. Sorting information simply means rearranging it in a different way. You can rearrange tables alphabetically, numerically, or by date. And you can sort tables in ascending or descending order.

This is best illustrated by example. Let's say you wanted to sort the list shown here alphabetically by last name, in ascending order:

Last Name	First Name	Age	Patient ID	Length of Stay
Castorp	Hans L.	27	ISB-2939	7
Settembrini	Ludovico	42	ISB-2443	9
Peeperkorn	Pieter	dec.	ISB-3325	1
Chauchat	Clavdia	26	ISB-2449	8
Ziemssen	Joachim	dec.	ISB-2845	2
Ferge	Anton K.	35	ISB-3038	4
Stohr	Caroline	33	ISB-2367	8

To sort a list like this one:

1 Select *all* columns and rows that you wish to sort.

A common mistake is to include the headings in the sort. Excel is smart enough not to sort the headings if they're obviously headings, but be careful. An even worse mistake is not choosing all the columns you wish to sort. If you don't sort all the columns at once, a sort can create fear and loathing.

2 Click the Sort Ascending button on the Standard toolbar. Excel will sort your data alphabetically, in ascending order. Your list will look like this.

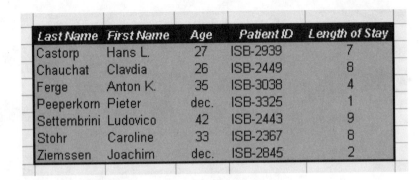

Last Name	First Name	Age	Patient ID	Length of Stay
Castorp	Hans L.	27	ISB-2939	7
Chauchat	Clavdia	26	ISB-2449	8
Ferge	Anton K.	35	ISB-3038	4
Peeperkorn	Pieter	dec.	ISB-3325	1
Settembrini	Ludovico	42	ISB-2443	9
Stohr	Caroline	33	ISB-2367	8
Ziemssen	Joachim	dec.	ISB-2845	2

Had you wanted to sort alphabetically in *descending* order, you could have clicked the Sort Descending button in the Standard toolbar.

You can perform much more sophisticated sorts by using the Sort menu command:

1 Select the range you wish to sort.

2 Choose Data ➤ Sort. The Sort dialog box appears:

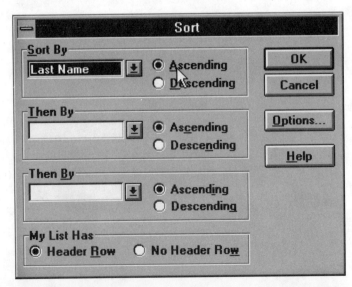

3 Excel automatically inserts the first column's heading into the Sort By box. If you want to sort by a different column (in the example shown below, the sort is being done by age), just click the down-arrow to see a list of possible sort indexes:

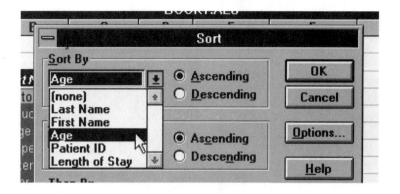

You can then go to the Then By fields if you want to have secondary or tertiary search indexes, and sort by them as well. You would have a secondary index, for example, if you were sorting a list and several people on it had the same last name. In that case, you would sort by last name and *then by* first name, so that Martinez, Charles came before Martinez, Michele.

4 Choose a Then By field, if necessary.

5 When you are finished, click OK.

See Also Selecting

SPELLING CHECKER

You can check the spelling of text in your worksheets with the Spelling utility. The *spelling checker* is fairly intuitive and can even offer suggestions for unfamiliar words.

To check the spelling in a worksheet:

1 Start the spelling checker using one of these techniques:

- ✓ Click the Spelling button on the Standard toolbar
- ✓ Choose Tools ➤ Spelling
- ✓ Press F7

The Spelling dialog box will appear and find the first unfamiliar word:

	Spelling	
Not in Dictionary: Castorp		
Change To: Castorp		
Suggestions:	Ignore	Ignore All
Castor	Change	Change All
Castors		
Castro		
Caster		
Catsup	Add	Suggest
Chastener		
Add Words To: CUSTOM.DIC		
Cell Value: Castorp		
☒ Always Suggest		
☐ Ignore UPPERCASE	Undo Last	Cancel	Help

2 You have several options at this point:

> **Ignore** Continues the spelling check without making changes.

> **Ignore All** Continues without changes and ignores any other occurrences of the unfamiliar word.

> **Change** Changes the word to a correction that you have typed or to a word that Excel has suggested.

> **Change All** Changes the word to a correction that you have typed or to a word that Excel has suggested, and changes all other occurrences of the word the same way.

> **Add** Appends a word to the custom dictionary.

> **Suggest** Suggests words that are spelled similarly.

> **Undo Last** Undoes your most recent change.

3 Clicking any button except Suggest or Undo Last takes you to the next unknown word, where you just repeat step 2.

4 When the Spelling checker reaches the end of the worksheet, a dialog box comes up asking if you want to continue checking from the beginning. Click either Yes or No.

SPLITTING WINDOWS

There will be times when you want to see widely separated areas of a worksheet. Scrolling between the different parts can be a bother, not to mention ineffective. That's when you want to *split* your windows. Splitting windows simply means dividing the worksheet in half (or in quarters) and having each half of the screen show different parts of the worksheet.

To split a window:

1 Either choose Window ➤ Split or drag one of the split boxes in one of the scroll bars. A split box is the small black box above or to the right of the arrows in the scroll bar. When the mouse cursor is over a split box, it looks like this:

April	Total
26258	179602
37354	152650
74154	209547

If you use the menu, the window will split horizontally. You can split windows horizontally, vertically, or both ways with the mouse method.

2 If you want to split the window into quarters, drag the other split box.

To unsplit a window, either drag the split box, double-click on the split box, or choose Window ➤ Unsplit.

See Also Freezing Panes, Multiple Worksheets

You must *start* Excel (put it into RAM) before you can use the program. There are four ways to start Excel from the Windows Program Manager:

- Double-click the Excel icon:

Microsoft
Excel

- Double-click on a file created in Excel.
- Choose File ➤ Run, and type **Excel** in the Command Line box. When you click OK, Excel will start up.
- Place Excel in your StartUp group. If you do this, Excel will start up automatically when you start Windows.

See Also   Open

STATUS BAR

The area along the bottom of the screen is called the *status bar*. The status bar is an information area that tells you about whatever happens to be going on in Excel. For example, when you highlight a menu option or position the cursor over a

toolbar button, information about the menu option or button appears in the status bar:

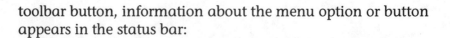

Saves changes made to active document   NUM

The right side of the status bar tells you whether Num Lock, Caps Lock, or Scroll Lock is on.

TABS

See Sheet Tabs.

TIME

See Date and Time.

TIPWIZARD

Excel "watches" you as you work in Big Brotherly fashion. In fact, that humming you hear from your computer is virtual giggling. Seriously, because Excel monitors all your activity (mouse-clicks, menu choices, etc.), it can often make helpful suggestions for easier or quicker ways to perform certain actions.

When Excel has something to tell you, the TipWizard button in the Standard toolbar turns yellow. Click on it to bring up the TipWizard bar (it appears just above the formula bar) and read the advice Excel has for you. Click the TipWizard button again to remove the TipWizard bar.

See Also   Help

TOOLBARS

Many of Excel's commands can be found in button form on its many *toolbars*. Toolbars are collections of shortcut buttons, lists, and palettes that you can use to edit or format worksheets. The advantage of using toolbars over menu commands is that you can often save yourself the trouble of making several different menu selections.

To execute the command associated with a toolbar button, just click that button. By holding the cursor over the button, you can make its menu name appear:

Common Excel toolbars include:

Standard   Here you will find many of the File and Edit menu commands, including Save, Open, Print, Cut, and Paste, as well as Help and several utilities.

Formatting   Offers many useful formatting commands, including Bold, Italic, alignment options, number style, and several palettes.

Chart   Offers five of the basic chart commands, including Chart Type and ChartWizard.

Drawing Offers all the tools you use for drawing objects on your worksheets, including lines, shapes, and arrows.

Visual Basic Offers the commands you use when creating macros.

The inside back cover of this book shows some toolbars with their buttons labeled.

You can click on toolbars and drag them anywhere on the screen. You can often resize the toolbar to a different shape to make it easier to work with. For instance, if you drag the Standard toolbar down, it looks like this:

Once you've dragged the toolbar down, click the small Close box in the upper-left corner to get rid of it. Double-click the toolbar to send it to the top of the screen. You can double-click a toolbar that is at the top of the screen to make it move down.

You can also control which toolbars are showing from a dialog box:

1 Choose View ➤ Toolbars. The Toolbars dialog box appears.

2 Click to place an *X* next to the toolbars you want to see on screen. You can also play with these options:

> **Color Toolbars** Displays the toolbars in color.

> **Large Buttons** Makes the buttons larger. Note that if you choose Large Buttons, fewer buttons will be visible on your toolbars.

3 When you are satisfied, click OK. Any toolbars you have indicated will appear on the screen.

See Also Charts, Drawing, Formatting, Macros

Undo/Redo

Often when you make a mistake you can *undo* it if you use the Undo command immediately. You can even undo your undo if you use Redo immediately. Both commands reside on the Edit menu, and their names change depending on what you've just done.

To undo a command or action, use one of these methods:

- Click the Undo button on the Standard toolbar
- Choose Edit ➤ Undo *action*
- Press Ctrl+Z

If an action or command cannot be undone, the command will be dimmed and will display *Can't Undo*.

Many actions are *not* undoable. So don't go around blithely sorting, spell checking, etc. without first giving some thought to whether your next action is undoable and how much agony it would cause if you screwed up. Undo is a good friend, but like most friends, it's reliable only under certain circumstances.

To redo a command or action, use one of these methods:

- Click the Redo button on the Standard toolbar (it looks like the Undo button)
- Choose Edit ➤ Redo (u) *action*
- Press Ctrl+Z

If an action or command cannot be redone, the command will be dimmed and will display *Can't Redo*.

See Also   Repeat

VALUES

Values is a general term for the numbers in a worksheet that are not used in formulas. The results of formulas, though, are values. Usually values represent amounts—money, inventory, ages, dates, percentages, and so on.

Several buttons on the Formatting toolbar can be used to format values in a worksheet:

Currency Style   Places a dollar sign in front of numbers. Depending upon other settings, it might also add commas and *.00* at the end if no cents are specified.

Percent Style Places a percent sign next to each number, converting it from a raw number to a percent. For example, if you type in *30* and then click the Percent Style button, your value will read *3000%*. Oops! What you probably wanted was *30%*, in which case you must enter the original number as *.30*.

Comma Style Places commas in numbers and, depending upon other settings, might also place commas and *.00* at the end if no cents are specified.

Increase Decimal Adds one decimal place to the value for each click. Note that this adds zeroes, not numbers, if there is no *mantissa* (numbers after the decimal place).

Decrease Decimal Removes one decimal place from the value for each click. Note that this does not delete the mantissa if there is one; rather, it just prevents it from showing. Furthermore, once you are down to the *characteristic* (numbers preceding the decimal place) part of the value, Decrease Decimal has no effect.

There are literally dozens of different number styles. You can select one by choosing Format ➤ Cells (or pressing Ctrl+1). In the Format Cells dialog box, you can choose from a number of categories in the Number tab, which displays categories along with their format codes.

See Also　Data, Formatting

WIZARDS

A wizard is a magical being that leaps out of LPT1 (Leprechaun Protocol Terminus 1) and turns you into a frog. No, that isn't true. And there's no Easter bunny, either.

Excel's *wizards* are utilities that simplify common tasks, such as creating charts or functions. There are three wizards:

　ChartWizard

　Function Wizard

　TipWizard

Each has its own button on the Standard toolbar and is discussed in detail in its own section. Why is there a space in Function Wizard? I haven't a clue.

Generally, wizards work as follows:

1 You bring up the wizard by clicking its button on the Standard toolbar.

2 You are taken through several dialog boxes, where you are asked to help the wizard out or choose default settings.

3 When you close the wizard by clicking the Finish button, it does what you've asked it to do.

See Also　ChartWizard, Function Wizard, TipWizard

WORKBOOKS

In Excel, entire files are termed *workbooks.* A workbook is a collection of worksheets, charts, and any other objects you have inserted, such as pictures. By default, new workbooks have 16 worksheets. You move between the worksheets of a workbook with the sheet tabs.

See Also New, Open, Sheet Tabs, Worksheets

WORKSHEET TABS

See Sheet tabs.

WORKSHEETS

In Excel, entire files are termed *workbooks,* and all Excel workbooks are divided into *worksheets.* By default, new workbooks have 16 worksheets. By having interconnected worksheets, Excel workbooks are three-dimensional. You move between the worksheets of a workbook with the sheet tabs.

Generally, you can do anything with worksheets that you do with rows and columns: you can insert worksheets, add or delete them, move them, format them, select them, etc.

See Also Freezing Panes, Moving between Worksheets, Multiple Worksheets, Sheet Tabs, Splitting Windows, Workbooks

ZOOM

What if you want to get a broad overview of your worksheet without splitting windows? Or suppose you want to get up close and personal? Either way, what you want to do in these situations is called *zooming,* I guess because you zoom in (getting closer) and out (getting farther away) as if you were on an electric camera.

To zoom in or out, use one of these techniques:

- Choose View ➤ Zoom and double-click on one of the percentages.

- Click on the Zoom Control list in the Standard toolbar and select one of the zoom percentages there:

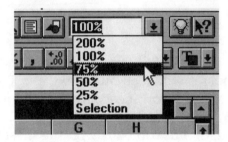

Notice that if you use very high or very low zoom percentages, items in your worksheet will grow or shrink to absurd proportions:

You might find this helpful, though, if you have a vision problem.

See Also   Splitting Windows

Index

Note to the Reader: Throughout this index, **boldfaced** page numbers indicate primary discussions of a topic. *Italicized* page numbers indicate illustrations.

C

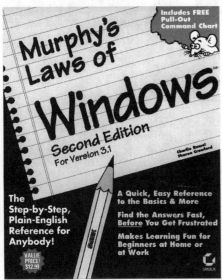

YES, YOU *CAN* DO WINDOWS.

964 pp. ISBN:842-4.

Mastering *Windows 3.1* is the most comprehensive start-to-finish Windows tutorial available today. And this Special Edition includes a special section that includes tips, tricks, and troubleshooting advice that alone is worth the price of the book.

Plus full coverage of all of the basics of Windows. Find out how to set up your desktop for ease of use, manipulate multiple windows and applications and more. You'll also find out about supercharging your system, running both Windows and DOS applications on your Windows 3.1 system.

There is also extensive coverage of advanced techniques, including TrueType font management, Dynamic Data Exchange (DDE) and Object Linking and Embedding (OLE) and multimedia support.

SYBEX. Help Yourself.

2021 Challenger Drive
Alameda, CA 94501
1-800-227-2346

SYBEX

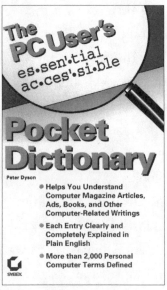

YOUR GUIDE TO A WORLD OF CONVENIENCE.

321 pp. ISBN: 798-3.

Finally there's a guide that helps you fulfill the promises of computer convenience you've always heard about — *Exploring the World of Online Services.*

With the help of this book, you can discover the myriad conveniences you can enjoy by using your computer and a modem. Find out how to send electronic mail and messages, or tap into over 5,500 public online databases. Get money-saving advice for choosing modems and communication software, and for saving money on your online bills.

Online veterans will especially enjoy the in-depth coverage of WinCIM, the new Windows version of the CompuServe Information Manager (CIM), and the in-depth discussion of a range of online service providers.

SYBEX. Help Yourself.

2021 Challenger Drive
Alameda, CA 94501
800-227-2346

SYBEX

GET A FREE CATALOG JUST FOR EXPRESSING YOUR OPINION.

Help us improve our books and get a *FREE* full-color catalog in the bargain. Please complete this form, pull out this page and send it in today. The address is on the reverse side.

Name _____   Company _____

Address _____   City _____ State ____ Zip _____

Phone ( )_____

1. How would you rate the overall quality of this book?

❑ Excellent
❑ Very Good
❑ Good
❑ Fair
❑ Below Average
❑ Poor

2. What were the things you liked most about the book? (Check all that apply)

❑ Pace
❑ Format
❑ Writing Style
❑ Examples
❑ Table of Contents
❑ Index
❑ Price
❑ Illustrations
❑ Type Style
❑ Cover
❑ Depth of Coverage
❑ Fast Track Notes

3. What were the things you liked *least* about the book? (Check all that apply)

❑ Pace
❑ Format
❑ Writing Style
❑ Examples
❑ Table of Contents
❑ Index
❑ Price
❑ Illustrations
❑ Type Style
❑ Cover
❑ Depth of Coverage
❑ Fast Track Notes

4. Where did you buy this book?

❑ Bookstore chain
❑ Small independent bookstore
❑ Computer store
❑ Wholesale club
❑ College bookstore
❑ Technical bookstore
❑ Other _____

5. How did you decide to buy this particular book?

❑ Recommended by friend
❑ Recommended by store personnel
❑ Author's reputation
❑ Sybex's reputation
❑ Read book review in _____
❑ Other _____

6. How did you pay for this book?

❑ Used own funds
❑ Reimbursed by company
❑ Received book as a gift

7. What is your level of experience with the subject covered in this book?

❑ Beginner
❑ Intermediate
❑ Advanced

8. How long have you been using a computer?

years _____

months _____

9. Where do you most often use your computer?

❑ Home
❑ Work

❑ Both
❑ Other _____

10. What kind of computer equipment do you have? (Check all that apply)

❑ PC Compatible Desktop Computer
❑ PC Compatible Laptop Computer
❑ Apple/Mac Computer
❑ Apple/Mac Laptop Computer
❑ CD ROM
❑ Fax Modem
❑ Data Modem
❑ Scanner
❑ Sound Card
❑ Other _____

11. What other kinds of software packages do you ordinarily use?

❑ Accounting
❑ Databases
❑ Networks
❑ Apple/Mac
❑ Desktop Publishing
❑ Spreadsheets
❑ CAD
❑ Games
❑ Word Processing
❑ Communications
❑ Money Management
❑ Other _____

12. What operating systems do you ordinarily use?

❑ DOS
❑ OS/2
❑ Windows
❑ Apple/Mac
❑ Windows NT
❑ Other _____

13. On what computer-related subject(s) would you like to see more books?

_____

_____

_____

_____

14. Do you have any other comments about this book? (Please feel free to use a separate piece of paper if you need more room)

_____

_____

_____

_____

- - - - - - - - - - - - - - PLEASE FOLD, SEAL, AND MAIL TO SYBEX - - - - - - - - - - - -

SYBEX INC.
Department M
2021 Challenger Drive
Alameda, CA
94501

This Book Is Only the Beginning.